GREATER
LATE THAN
NEVER

GREATER LATE THAN NEVER

Fulfilling Your Dreams After 50

ROBERT E. HOPE

LONGSTREET
Atlanta, Georgia

Published by
LONGSTREET PRESS INC.
A subsidiary of Cox Newspapers,
A subsidiary of Cox Enterprises, Inc.
2140 Newmarket Parkway
Suite 122
Marietta, GA 30067

Printed in the United States of America
1st printing, 1998
Library of Congress Catalog Card Number: 97-76255
ISBN: 1-56352-470-8

Jacket and book design by Burtch Bennett Hunter

To Paul Beckham,
my business partner, who works each day with me
on my adventures into new ventures.
Together, we bring more than a hundred years
of experience to anything we do.

I appreciate and thank all the people I've met and discovered in
the process of writing this book. They are people who never grow
old and keep their lives focused on their futures.
I also appreciate my family, which has tolerated and accepted
my journeys in life that have frequently been motivated
by trying new things when doing the same old thing
might have been easier on all of us.

CONTENTS

GREATER
LATE THAN
NEVER

GETTING OLDER AND GIVING UP AREN'T THE SAME THING

Some people begin winding down when they turn 50 while others are just getting started.

While one person dreams of a day with no plan or alarm clock, another wants to climb the highest peaks or start a new business. While one wants to tinker and putter in a self-absorbed world, another is reaching out to new people and new horizons.

A mere century ago, most people couldn't expect to live to be 50. Life was fraught with risk of disease and war. Many jobs were extremely dangerous, and once someone was cast into a role in life, escape was difficult. Access to knowledge was limited, and many people could never dream of a better life or conceive of the wonders that they might want to reach out for.

Things are different today. Now, 50-year-olds run marathons, climb mountains, take up new careers, and have kids. This new expanded lifetime can be a real adventure. You could get lucky like Jeanne Calmet, the French woman who said on her 120th birthday, "God has forgotten me." Unlike most of us who worry about our weight and health, Ms. Calmet ate two pounds of chocolate a week and smoked until she was 117.

Making the most out of the years after 50 isn't a completely new idea. Ordinary people throughout history have stepped forward late in life to do extraordinary things. If they hadn't spent their final years in pursuit of greatness, they would have left no life record beyond a gravestone.

Growing old isn't unique. Right now, about four million Americans are turning age 50 every year. That's about one every seven seconds and more than 10,000 every day.

Many baby boomers fight age. In fact, the average 50-year-old views himself or herself as being 15 years younger. They are stunned when they meet someone the same age who has gray hair and wrinkles or realize an old codger finished only a year or two ahead of them in school.

Aging isn't easy. As the venerable late manager of the New York Mets, Casey Stengel, once said, "I'll never make the mistake of being 70 again."

For a moment, let's face the harshest reality of life: you're going to die. Now that the shock is over, don't take your impending death too seriously. Sooner or later it's going to happen. A lot of people will be sad. Some will be surprised, regardless of how much warning you may give them. Death is a once-in-a-lifetime experience, and it is a stunner.

My father had cancer for months. When we checked him into a hospital, the doctors told us he would die within days.

Dad surprised us all. He could no longer speak, could hardly see, and every move he made was a struggle. However, he insisted on leaving the hospital to go home one more time.

Back home, although doctors had predicted he wouldn't survive even the 20-minute ambulance trip, Dad asked me to go to the store and get him paints, brushes, and a canvas. He had dabbled as an artist for years and wanted to paint again.

Over the next several weeks, he would tediously paint a scene from a photo he had taken of a stream in the North Georgia mountains. He would paint for several minutes, then fall back exhausted in the hospital bed. A little while later he would be up painting again.

I went by to visit him every night after work for the next year. Writing notes back and forth, my father convinced me to take a new job and move my family to New York. He felt he had missed out on an opportunity in his life when he turned down a job in St. Paul twenty years earlier.

I started commuting to New York from Atlanta and checked in with him every day. Several times during the year, we had false alarms. We thought he was on the verge of dying, but he hung in and kept going.

When I was told in my New York apartment that he had died, I was stunned, caught totally by surprise. In truth, there could have been no greater warning. There really is no way to be ready.

From watching Dad's heroic effort to get the most out of his remaining days, I vowed that I would never waste even a moment. That's the spirit that's needed to keep living and accomplishing things past 50.

More so than death, life is a very serious matter. Sadly, not everyone takes it that way. Some people, as they get older, seem to take their lives for granted.

It is what you do now in this precious time you have left to live that counts. It's all you've got for the moment. And it's not going to get any easier.

Albert Einstein once said that his Theory of Relativity was simple. "Relativity," he noted, "is why a minute talking to your old maid aunt seems like an hour while an hour with a beautiful girl seems like a minute."

Relativity in this book is making the most of time. It is making sure that the last moments of life are as exciting as the earlier ones and that the best times are savored.

This book was inspired by my turning age 50. The year 1996 holds great significance to me. It was the year of the Olympics in Atlanta, where I live. It was also the year of a national presidential election. Some things that happened in 1996 will probably last for a long time in history books, but for me the most monumental event was my birthday.

No longer can I think of myself as young. In my mid-40s, I saw myself as little different than in my mid-20s. I was young even if I didn't look that way. Suddenly, almost overnight, too many people I work with are younger than I am. My youthful perspective on matters has become sage advice.

People who look the age I envisioned myself just a year or two ago call me "sir." In fact, lots of people call me sir. I get far too much respect from adults. I resent it.

When I go to football games or concerts, no one gets rowdy with me. If I demand that someone put out his cigarette because the smoke is bothering me, he doesn't get mad and threaten to hit me. Younger folks act as if they are concerned about my health. They treat me with respect, like an old man.

When I'm in New York on business, I go to the health club in the Waldorf-Astoria to exercise. I consider myself somewhat of a seniors champion on the Stairmaster. Youngsters watch in awe as I climb continuously for hours, going nowhere. At the Waldorf health club, I want to strike back each time the supervisor comes up to me and asks, "Are you OK, sir?"

I smile and nod, but I want to say, "Of course, I'm OK. I came here to exercise and sweat and that's exactly what I'm doing. Stop asking."

My hair is thinner. It's getting gray on the edges. My stomach bulges, and my eyes are growing blurry. I'm not ready for all this. I go to the Y three times a week and work out as hard as I ever have in my life. But nothing seems to happen to my body. I plunge ahead, fearing what I might look like if I stopped.

So, this is aging? It must be, but I'm not totally ready to accept it. I want to keep dreaming, and not dwell on memories. I'll occasionally catch myself telling stories of the "old days" to the young people in the office, but I want to keep doing things that become new stories. I don't want the stories to end.

The inspiration to write *Greater Late Than Never* was the second epiphany of the first year of my second half-century. The first came several months earlier when I tried out for a local production of a Broadway musical. What moved me to show up at the audition is beyond me. I can't sing. I can't dance. But, it seemed now or never. I really wanted the part, and the bigger the better.

I got the lead. I was Nathan Detroit in a Stone Mountain, Georgia, production of *Guys and Dolls*. I did things I had never done in my life. Yes, I sang "Sue Me" and an assortment of other songs. I crawled across the stage after the lovely Adelaide. I wore loud gangster suits and makeup. I even embraced and kissed Adelaide right in front of the world. I loved it.

It was an amazing experience for me. I hadn't tried to memorize anything longer than a phone number since the required reciting of poetry in high school English. I was very proud that I could remember all the lines in a play. Memorizing and acting were adventures I'd never pursued.

And, by the way, I know that I was the star of a very local community theater production and that the talent pool available wasn't huge. However, my innermost feeling was that I might have been the best Nathan Detroit of all time.

Once I won the part, I tried to recruit some of my friends to be gangsters in the show with me. My brother-in-law, Don, pitched right in. He had a great time, too. The whole process of rehearsing, changing scenes and outfits, coming on stage left or right, entering at the right time, and adjusting to the flubs of others — it was all new to us.

While I was getting ready for my role as Nathan Detroit, most people made friendly comments, laughing and having a good time with me. However, one of my friends had a different way of looking at it.

"Aren't you a little old to be getting into something like this?" he asked. "What is this, your midlife crisis?"

I hadn't thought much about why I was doing it until that moment. He was right. It was some kind of middle-age craziness that had come over me. However, I really liked it. For all the hard work put into it, I didn't want the show to end. I had conquered something inside me that I didn't know I could. I was pleased with myself and had made new friends.

I started a project at a time in my life when the idea of standing in front of a crowd and singing was unimaginable and scared me. I had never done it and would have felt awkward and stupid if I had tried.

Me (left) as Nathan Detroit in *Guys and Dolls*

My first attempt, the words would hardly come out. The efforts to sing were feeble and the sounds weird. By the time the show ran, as if by magic, I could stand up and belt out the words without much thought at all. What a transformation! One giant step for Bob, somewhat of a minor stumble for American theater. An old man did something new . . . and was proud.

The writing of this book is a retooling of my life. It is a process of seeking evidence and proving that good things can be on the horizon after age 50 and that all I lived for is not behind me. It is a reason not to look at the obituaries in the newspaper but to see how old someone is when he or she does something remarkable.

It has surprised me how many times someone was a nobody and then became a somebody after age 50. Not all were admirable. However, they were remarkable. Carlo Gambino bumped off his rival at age 55 to take control of what became the notorious Gambino Family. Even such a bad thing becomes a little more proof that time can be a friend. Carlo died of natural causes at age 75.

This is a book about people whose lives, like mine, blended in with everyone else's. The world had no reason to notice them. They were good people leading ordinary lives. There is nothing wrong with ordinary, but this book is driven by those who dreamed to be extraordinary.

After 50, they shocked the world. They did something remarkable.

Others in the book went from one domain of greatness to a new arena. In some cases, people who achieve fame and fortune early find a path to something else that is more important to them later in life. If being outstanding once is hard, being great in two different careers is pretty incredible. It happens.

At a time when Princess Diana's untimely death brought universal mourning, it is all too obvious that youth and beauty are overpowering qualities today. When Mother Teresa died, her good deeds were not enough to capture the same interest.

In most ways, the world belongs to the young. However, some people overcome youth and outlive it in every sense. To quote Dorothy Fuldheim, "This is a youth-oriented society, and the joke is on them because youth is a disease from which we all recover."

Some step up in their later years and make people know they count. They make us pay attention. They accomplish something special when their times at bat are running out and most of the people their age have quit reaching for the sky.

If I am to do anything great, it will be in some future year. Just knowing that other people have done great things after age 50 inspires and pleases me. Life is not just for the young but also the young at heart. There are plenty of examples.

Two of the most influential humans in history — Muhammad and Confucius — both got started late in life. Confucius was fired at 50.

Muhammad was a businessman who became fed up with religion and started his own at about the same age.

Others just didn't like what they were doing and changed.

John Newton was a sea captain who dealt in human cargo. At age 82, he convinced Parliament to abolish the slave trade in the British Empire. He also wrote the hymn that is now the most popular piece of religious music in the world, "Amazing Grace."

We find business successes like Ray Kroc. He was selling milkshake mixers when he had the idea at age 50 of opening restaurants. He built McDonald's.

In sports, Tom Wargo was a blue-collar worker who enjoyed golf. He took a year off to polish his game and joined the Senior PGA Tour at 50, becoming one of the best.

Some are famous and some are not. An actress started a wildlife preserve after 50, and a golfer, on his 72nd birthday, broke the course record of a legend. A Hall of Fame pitcher took on the cause of giving little girls a chance to play baseball, his sport. A 105-year-old aerobics teacher and a 94-year-old doctor defied time.

Some could be a little nuts. A 50-year-old actress painted in the nude with her body and a 60-year-old went out for college football.

What do all of them have in common? Why do they speed up when others their age are slowing down? Why do they continue trying to accomplish something and be somebody? When does old start being old and young stop being young, and why is it a different age in different people?

When the two-minute warning of life sounds, some people have stopped trying and might as well be out of the game. Others use every minute, call every time-out, and make the most of every final second. I want to be on their team.

FINISHING LIFE IN A BLAZE OF GLORY

My favorite character in history is John Newton.

Most people haven't heard of him, and I wouldn't have either if it hadn't been for Alex Haley, the author of *Roots*.

Haley lived in Knoxville, Tennessee, where I worked for three years and constantly heard stories about the famous author at parties and gatherings. One friend moved into a home that had belonged to Haley and told how Haley had a huge stained-glass church window that covered most of the front of the house. My friend was Jewish and had the window removed.

Another story was about Haley's final project — the one that died with him.

He wanted to do a movie on the life of John Newton.

Newton grew up in England in the 1700s as the son of a sea captain. His mother wanted him to become a vicar in the Church of England. His father wanted him to follow in his footsteps and go to sea.

When John was 12, his mother died. John became an apprentice on a cargo ship.

He eventually became a sea captain himself. Like most people who have good jobs and a good life, John may have occasionally lusted to do something else but was basically pretty happy. He'd deliver whatever cargo was assigned to him to whatever port of call it was addressed. He kept his excellent writing skills, gained through his mother's teaching, and polished by updating his ship's log daily while at sea.

John Newton

A fine captain. A noble occupation.

Only, John Newton saw something that troubled him.

He was assigned slaves as a cargo, with ports of call in the colonies and England. In the colonies, the slaves harvested fields of cotton and tobacco. The rationale was that they were treated well, given housing, food and clothing, and were probably better off than they were in the wilds of the African jungle. Lots of people were needed to work the plantations, and slave labor seemed to be the only economical approach to getting it done.

Newton could accept the logic of why slaves were needed in America, but he didn't buy what he saw in England. Slaves in England weren't needed for farming. They were treated as pets. Stature of noblemen was based on the number of lackeys who accompanied their carriages, running alongside as they traveled. Deformed or particularly nice-looking slaves were frequently put on leashes and shown off as the aristocracy walked with them through London streets.

Then Newton got to know slaves on the ship he captained. Sometimes workers who were taken from the jungles would work for the slave-trading companies, learn English, and later be shipped and sold abroad. It was easy to befriend these individuals. He heard stories of groups of slaves who would jump overboard in their chains rather than leave their homeland under force.

John Newton decided to do something about it.

He decided to take the route that his mother preferred for his life. He went to the Church of England and applied to be a vicar. Initially, he was denied because of his age. Anyone past 40 had limited options. When he was finally accepted, he was told he would be assigned to a small rural parish and would have little chance to move to a bigger church.

Newton was opposed to slavery and eager to tell anyone who would listen. At first, few did. Few in England saw anything wrong with what was happening in that country. The slaves lived in homes and were treated well. Frequently, they did no work. They certainly were in no danger. Newton's conviction was regarded as odd and meaningless.

One day, he and his friend, noted poet William Cowpers, decided to hold their own hymn-writing contest: Who could write the words to a hymn the fastest? Who won the speed portion of the contest was never recorded, but Newton definitely won on content. He wrote a quick ditty to a British pub tune. It was a short autobiography of his life that he titled "Amazing Grace."

"Amazing Grace, how sweet the sound that saved a wretch like me. I once was lost but now am found, was blind but now I see." It was the story of a slave ship captain who changed his ways.

The words swept through England, and Newton's new celebrity status paid off. Since the opinions of famous people are generally viewed as more important than those of common people, his messages against slavery began to influence his audiences.

It took John Newton forty years to build momentum for his cause. His last speech was his greatest.

In 1811, he stood before Parliament at age 82 to plead his case for abolishing slavery. He was weak and sick. He couldn't finish and was helped from the podium. But, he made his point. Parliament voted to outlaw the transport and trade of slaves within the British Empire, which created the domino effect that finally halted the slave trade throughout the world.

Newton died a few months later.

I like John Newton because his life was always ahead of him. He wrote "Amazing Grace" at age 50 (which was the life expectancy of the average male in his day). Up until that point, he had done nothing to warrant much attention. Then, moved to action by his conviction, he went full-speed ahead for thirty-two more years. Like a rocket in a fireworks show, he kept rising and rising, and boom, the biggest blast happened at the end.

BILL McCARTNEY

The Colorado Buffaloes defeated Notre Dame in the Orange Bowl and closed their 1990 season as college football's national champions. Just four years earlier, the team had only won one game. The Buffaloes' coach was Bill McCartney — age 50. McCartney had been at the school for years, and his team was the best in the school's history. After the 1989 season, when the Buffaloes went to the Orange Bowl but lost, McCartney was awarded a fifteen-year coaching contract. Things could hardly look better for the school's football program.

Unexpectedly, Bill McCartney resigned.

Fans of the team knew that the 1989 season was particularly difficult for him. His star quarterback, Sal Aunese, died of cancer during the first month of the season. At the funeral, McCartney, a very religious man, announced that his daughter was pregnant out of wedlock and that Aunese was the father of the child. But things seemed to have settled down and were going smoothly in 1990.

When McCartney resigned, he announced no plans, only that he had good relationships with his coaches, the school administration, and his players. There was no problem with the school or the job.

He just needed to spend more time with his family.

In 1990, McCartney founded a Christian-based organization of men called the Promise Keepers with a primary goal of building the right relationships in the home.

By the end of 1990, Promise Keepers had 4,000 members. The group started holding meetings in stadiums across the country. The stadiums became packed. By 1994, Promise Keepers had 278,000 members.

A crowd of 72,548 showed up in 1995 for a Promise Keepers event at the Los Angeles Coliseum. A meeting at the Pontiac Silverdome in Michigan drew 70,490. Hundreds of thousands of men appeared at the group's first assembly in the nation's capital at the Washington Mall in 1997, and more than a million men participated in seminars throughout 1996.

The organization is built on seven promises that each of its members vows to keep:

- Honor Jesus Christ.
- Pursue vital relationships with a few other men.
- Practice spiritual, moral, ethical, and sexual purity.
- Build strong marriages and families through love, protection, and biblical values.
- Support your church.
- Reach beyond racial and denominational barriers.
- Influence the world by loving others and treating them with respect.

The organization is controversial and called chauvinistic by some, but no one questions McCartney's conviction and dedication to his cause. Bill McCartney moved from being a great coach late in his life to becoming a great leader of men and a powerful influence on the morals of the world.

JOE GIBBS

Another football coach took a totally different route.

Joe Gibbs was 52 years old and the most successful coach in the history of the Washington Redskins and the National Football League. In twelve seasons as head coach, he won four league championships and three Super Bowls. His name is in the NFL Hall of Fame.

In his first season as coach of the Redskins in 1981, he owed $1.2 million to seven banks from real estate investments that had gone bad. His team started its season that year without a win in the first five games.

Gibbs recalls, "I got on my knees and said, 'Hey, God, it's in your hands. I'm bankrupt. The only person who can straighten this out is you.' " The next season the Redskins won their first Super Bowl, and he was able to pay off his debts over a three-year period.

The bankruptcy burned in Gibbs a memory of poor judgments and misplaced trust. The security of coaching was important to him. But, contrary to all logic, after a successful 1993 season, Joe Gibbs quit football.

Gibbs' oldest son, J. D., had raced cars during school, and the entire Gibbs family enjoyed auto racing. Joe had "dabbled" in racing his last two years as a coach. He decided to make it his business.

He started Joe Gibbs Racing, which now has sixty employees and is opening a 124,000-square-foot facility in Charlotte, North Carolina, that will house the racing operation along with a museum and auditorium.

Gibb's relationship with his family had a lot to do with his change.

His wife, Pat, had two operations for brain tumors in 1979. She was fully recovered before he became coach of the Redskins in 1981, but he cherished spending time with her and his two sons. The life of a football coach didn't allow for that. Seven months of the year he lived and breathed football and was in complete isolation from his family.

In football, the only time Pat joined him for a weekend game was the Super Bowl. As head of Joe Gibbs Racing, he also travels on weekends to races, but Pat goes along. Also, Joe, J. D., and Coy Gibbs are all working together every day at Joe Gibbs Racing. Joe and Pat own 52 percent of the racing operation, and J. D. and Coy own the rest.

Joe Gibbs

Gibbs was at the top in his football career, but the top wasn't what he expected. "People would tell me I had the greatest job in the world," he said, "but one day I woke up and looked at the upcoming football season and thought, 'I've climbed that mountain before.'"

"It was scary when I left football, but it was the right thing for me. It's given me a whole new look at life and has been invigorating. . . . Sometimes we're afraid to move in new directions, but I now know not to be afraid. For me, twenty-eight years of doing the same thing was enough. It's a new world for me and I'm still going for a championship."

TIPPI HEDREN

Actress Tippi Hedren arrived in Hollywood in 1960 with her baby daughter, Melanie. She was already a well-known New York model but had a goal of becoming a movie star. She succeeded. And eventually, so did her daughter, Melanie Griffith.

Tippi starred in the Alfred Hitchcock thrillers *The Birds* and *Marnie,* and was called "Hitchcock's newest find" in the *Saturday Review.* Hitchcock believed Tippi had "faster tempo, city glibness, more humor" than Grace Kelly.

A beautiful young, blonde actress, the rage of Hollywood: This is surely an achievement so great that the memories could sustain the aging woman.

Except that the woman had more to give. Today, at age 60, her passion isn't old movies and memories, but wild animals.

Tippi is founder and president of the Roar Foundation and lives on an 80-acre wildlife preservation called Shambala, surrounded by wild lions and other jungle animals.

Shambala is the only game preserve of its kind in the United States. Since 1972, it has provided a safe haven for exotic big cats. More than seventy live there, including lions, tigers, leopards, snow leopards, servals, mountain lions, and a Florida panther. A cheetah and two African elephants also live on the preserve.

Tippi established the Roar Foundation in 1983 as a nonprofit charitable organization, and the preserve is open to the public.

Still slim, attractive, and stylish, the classic movie star sits on her porch overlooking her family of animals gathered from circuses, zoos, and a variety of other sources. "To have something like this is a wild, crazy dream," she says. "It's also folly, because it takes so much money. But these animals are so much in my blood, my soul, that there's no way I could give them up."

Who said anything about giving up?

TOM WARGO

Golf was in Tom Wargo's soul.

The 50-year-old journeyman golfer was working as an attendant and part owner of a small golf club in Centralia, Illinois. Prior to that, he had been a steelworker, an auto worker, a bartender, and held an assortment of other odd jobs over the years. However, his first love was golf, but he was never good enough to consider going on the PGA Tour.

At 50, he had an idea. He was old enough to play on the Senior PGA Tour. He took a year and concentrated on polishing his golf. Unlike other pro golfers who grew up with the game and took hours and hours of instruction on its finer points, he had taught himself to play.

On April 18, 1993, in Palm Beach Gardens, Florida, Tom Wargo sank a four-foot putt in sudden death to win the PGA Senior Championship. For the last four years, he has been one of the top money-winners on the senior pro tour. A rough-looking, scrappy, and muscular man, he is the blue-collar worker on the white-shoe senior tour with such players as Trevino, Player, Weiskopf, Nicklaus, and Palmer, who have been household names in golf for years. He has turned a midlife crisis into a $3 million, four-year career on the pro circuit.

Waiting until late to be "great" can be a positive as far as character development is concerned. "Drunks are hard on you," Wargo says, recalling his days as a bartender. "Have you ever been in one of those old-fashioned roadhouses? You had to throw them out the door. I've always said that every young man should go through two things in his life: tending bar and going to jail for thirty days as I did. You learn a lot. And it sure makes you humble in a hurry.

"Some of these guys, I can't figure out what they're still doing out here," he said. "It puzzles me why they still go at it so hard. I plan to bust this a couple more years and then see where I stand. Right now, there are still some toys I want to buy.

"But what I want to do eventually is go back to the course in Centralia and brew up the coffee and stand in the pro shop and talk to the members. That's how I got into this, and that's how I want to go out."

"I don't think of myself as a club pro or a touring pro," he notes. "I'm just a player, trying to win a golf tournament the best way I can."

History is full of people like Tom Wargo, Joe Gibbs, Bill McCartney, Tippi Hedron, and John Newton — the ones who get better and stronger the longer they live. For all the enthusiasm of youth, the wisdom of age frequently comes through with remarkable achievements. Consider the following stories.

Winston Churchill

At middle age, his once promising political career had fallen into tatters. A nobleman, he grew up in a 360-room castle, served as his country's naval leader and First Lord of the Exchequer, and became an accomplished painter and historian. But then his policies fell out of favor, and he went into "a political wilderness." At age 66, he faced his greatest challenge and met it successfully. He became Prime Minister of Great Britain in 1940, and he led the free world through its "greatest hour." He coined the term "Iron Curtain," and he received his most colorful tribute in a message from President Roosevelt that read, "It is fun living in a century with you." He was the most remarkable statesman of the 20th Century.

Albert Einstein

A school dropout, young Albert didn't come to the United States until he was 40. Even though he did great work in his 20s, the genius we know is an old man who loved children and cared little for money, even turning down an offer to be president of Israel. His letter to President Roosevelt in 1939, written when he was 60 years old, convinced Roosevelt to initiate the development of the atomic bomb. That changed the nature of warfare forever.

Audrey Hepburn

Born in Brussels, Hepburn grew up in war-torn Holland during Hitler's invasion. Many of her family members were killed. After leaving Europe, she worked as a chorus girl before becoming one of the most popular actresses in American movies. Audrey Hepburn starred in such movies as *Breakfast at Tiffany's*, *Sabrina*, *My Fair Lady*, *Funny Face*, and *Roman*

Holiday. She was known by everyone, and her delicate beauty made her look fragile, maybe even weak. She wasn't. In 1988, at age 59, she became the chief spokesperson for the United Nations Children's Fund. She traveled to remote places like Somalia and Kenya to help impoverished children and traveled around the world to Nairobi, London, Geneva, Paris, New York, and other major cities to raise money and tell the press about UNICEF. She died in 1993, having devoted the final five years of her life to helping people suffering from war and poverty, as she had as a child.

Confucius

One of history's most influential thinkers, he set the philosophy that guided Chinese society for centuries. Fired from his job as a government accountant at age 50, he became a teacher — a very exceptional one.

Muhammad

One of the most important figures in world history, Muhammad was a businessman who at middle age wasn't satisfied with any of the religions that existed at the time. So he started his own. He founded Islam.

Moses

This revered religious figure was an old man who didn't feel up to the task at first when he led the Hebrews in their exodus from Egypt. The aging prophet is credited with writing the first five books of the Old Testament and his accomplishments are respected 3,200 years later by Christians, Moslems, and Jews.

Betty Ford

The First Lady of the United States overcame breast cancer, then later won her battle over an addiction to alcohol and pills. At age 62, she started the Betty Ford Center for people with alcohol and drug dependency. Located on fourteen acres in Rancho Mirage, California, it is the most famous treatment center in the world. The center has made us more aware of the problem of dependency, particularly in women, who were once frequently overlooked in treatment for addiction.

Mohandas K. Gandhi

A London-trained lawyer scrapped the trappings of his business life at age 50 to lead India to independence while living in poverty and wearing a simple loincloth. His doctrine of nonviolence influenced other leaders of civil freedom movements such as Martin Luther King, Jr., and Nelson Mandela.

Nelson Mandela

He started his battle to free blacks in South Africa at age 50. After spending more than twenty years in prison for his stance against apartheid, he was elected president of South Africa at age 76.

Johann Gutenberg

Popularly known as the inventor of the printing press, he actually invented movable type for use in printing. He printed the first Gutenberg Bible with his new invention when he was 54 years old.

Anna Mary Robertson Moses

She took up a career as an artist in 1938 at the age of 78, painting the scenes of her childhood. The wife of a dairy farmer, she started painting when her husband died and the farm life no longer took up so much of her time. At first, she sold her paintings in a drugstore for $5 each. She painted more than 1,500 pictures in the next twenty-three years. The most she ever personally received for a painting was $1,000, but she became famous throughout the world as Grandma Moses. An exhibit in Moscow in 1964 drew more than 100,000 visitors. "I look back on my life like a good day's work," she said. "It was done, and I feel satisfied with it. I was happy and contented. I knew nothing better and made the best out of what life offered. And life is what we make it, always has been and always will be."

Nicolaus Copernicus

In his 50s, he developed a new theory about the nature of the universe, surmising, in 1533, that the earth rotates on an axis, that the moon rotates around the earth, and that the earth and other planets revolve around the sun. He presented the theory in a series of lectures in Rome at age 60 and revolutionized the conception of the universe.

Golda Meir

She left a life as a Milwaukee schoolteacher to become Israel's first female prime minister at age 70. "I cannot say that women are better than men," she was quoted as saying. "However, I am certain they are no worse."

Pope John Paul II

He became pope at age 58 and is still going strong near age 80. Some jobs don't come early in life. Being pope is one of them.

William Harvey

An English physician, he wrote at age 50 a groundbreaking book in medical history. His *Anatomical Treatise on the Movement of the Heart and Blood in Animals* accurately described for the first time the function of the heart and circulatory system.

Louis Jacques Daguerre

At age 52 in 1839, the Frenchman announced his invention of photography.

Harry Truman

At 50, he had failed as an operator of a men's clothing store in Kansas City and had returned to farming. He then got into politics when he ran for civil court judge.

Ray Kroc

The founder of McDonald's was a high school dropout and a milkshake mixer salesman at age 50 when he decided to open a chain of fast-food restaurants.

Wilhelm Conrad Rontgen

The German scientist invented the X-ray machine in 1895 at age 50.

Gregory Pincus

The life of the American biologist was uneventful until he invented an oral contraceptive in 1956 at age 53. As much as any other discovery of the century, his work changed the world.

Madeleine Albright. Ben Franklin. Dwight Eisenhower. Ronald Reagan. Mother Teresa. George Washington. Casey Stengel. Eddie Robinson. Dr. Ruth. Colin Powell. Joe Paterno. Red Auerbach. Vince Lombardi. Eleanor Roosevelt. Pablo Picasso. This is an honor roll of senior citizens who shunned the idea that there is a time to start slowing down.

They kept going and never let age hold them back. Sometimes their lives were defined by one glorious moment. Others kept up a steady pace of achievement for years.

In every case, they made a difference at a time in life when others weren't even trying.

"Don't be afraid your life will end. Be afraid it will never begin."
— Grace Hansen

THE HARSH REALITY OF TIME

We get very excited when a baby is born. All kinds of plans are made to assure that the kid is treated well and goes to college and has a great career, a wonderful life. Some struggle during their life, some get rich, some achieve great things. All die.

Sue Beaumont of Chicago noted that seventeen of her friends were turning 50 in one year. She asked her friends to write something about being 50 in a book so she could give each a copy. Cindy Kinder, who had been sick much of her life with a rare blood disease, wrote, "I urge each one of you to enjoy each new day and make it a pleasant one . . . do something for yourself and live life to the fullest."

Cindy died before her 51st birthday.

Death is the great equalizer. What is done before death is what counts because it's all we have. It takes time to do something worthwhile, so it only makes sense to use all the time you've got. If you've delayed the action, start now.

When I was a young boy, I would go to bed and say my nightly prayer with a passion. "Now I lay me down to sleep, I pray the Lord my soul to keep; if I should die before I wake, I pray the Lord my soul to take." I'd pray with all my might that I wouldn't die. Death seemed so final.

When I was young, the only time that seemed important was the time of the moment. The only things that really seemed important were the things that were affecting my life. I was at the center of the world, and all lives and activities were a form of theater that was performing for my entertainment.

The whole concept of life ending was disconnected from my day-to-day life. When my grandfather, Pop, and grandmother, Mom, died, they were old and withered. Death was a shock but not a surprise. When I went to the funerals, I was 12. I peeked into the caskets just long enough to satisfy my mother and father. Then I left as quickly as I could. The viewing of corpses at funerals continued to scare me well into my adult life. It was the stuff of horror movies.

Pop was 72 but looked much older when he died. Mostly, he seemed to just sit in his big armchair and listen to the radio and later in his life, watch TV. Mom was 68 and also seemed very old. She died a few months after Pop. Both had heart attacks. I was told that Mom just lost her desire to live after Pop was gone, that she literally died of a broken heart. That sounded nice, but it was also perplexing. To think that someone would just fade away and finally die when a partner was gone left me with an uneasy feeling. Keeping a strong desire to stay alive meant a lot, I thought.

When I was in high school, the physical realities of the human body seemed out of sync with logic. Half of my long-time friends were girls. Suddenly they took on a new aura of sanctity and importance. They had something I didn't have that was the grandest of all prizes, if you believed what was being said in the movies and by the other guys.

Playboy magazine was just coming on the scene, and the centerfolds were a big topic for locker room discussion. We would sneak around and find copies to check out the photos, so mysterious and artistic. The women were perfect, just like plastic dolls.

It created an uneasy tension with the girls as we realized they possessed all the same equipment that we admired with such curiosity in a magazine. Guys would go out with particular girls and come back with stories that were too good to be true, which was usually the case.

At that time, the standard by which all females were physically measured was Marilyn Monroe. She was perfection, a "10."

One day, Marilyn Monroe unexpectedly died. Even worse, she committed suicide. I can remember walking to school — a trip that covered two miles and plenty of time to think — and trying to rationalize how a person with her looks could be gone. Her nude photos could still be found in our *Playboy* magazines, but she was gone from earth.

A few months later, I was playing table tennis in the school gym. An announcement came over the school public address system that President Kennedy had been shot. Again I was stunned that life was so tenuous and precious. The frivolity of life was being replaced by the serious issue that we weren't really immortal. Our time was limited, and if we had something we wanted to do, we'd better get going. Time would eventually run out.

In a way, life is like a vacation. It's only going to last a certain amount of time, and the key is to make the most of it.

Recently, my wife and I had dinner with five other couples at Bones, a fancy steak restaurant in Atlanta. We were celebrating the 50th birthday of my sister-in-law, Sandra Snow.

The dinner went on for hours as we talked about times that had come and gone.

I sat there thinking how much had happened over the past few years in our families. It didn't seem very long ago when we went to see Sandra's new baby girl. I sat in the living room of a small house, holding the baby while sitting on a sofa that was one of the few pieces of furniture in a very small living room.

The Snows have lived in three houses since, each bigger and more elaborate than the previous one. The baby is now married. Our baby who is the same age lives in a foreign land and is planning her wedding.

Someone finally mentioned the thought that arises at so many gatherings recently. "Remember when we were young and we thought 50 was so old? We don't seem that old."

"You'll be saying the same thing at 90," someone snapped back.

I never planned for life to happen this quickly.

Just when I'm getting started, I'm running out of time.

A 50-year-old male today has a life expectancy of just over twenty-one more years. Twenty-one years ago, I had two daughters, the same wife I have today, and lived in the same city. I had a lot of the same friends. Not much has changed in one sense, while a lot has changed in another.

Until recently, on my office wall I had a picture of my 8-year-old, looking up at the camera, smiling while making a snowman. Another photograph showed my 4-year-old standing in the ocean in her little two-piece bathing suit. When someone asked about my children, I proudly directed his gaze to the wall. A guest last year pointed out that I needed a new picture. I frankly didn't want a new picture. To me, my daughters seemed the same as they had been two brief decades before. Obviously, they are not.

I now have the photos of three adult women on my office wall — my wife and my children.

It has all sneaked up on me.

Most of my life happened while I was paying attention to other things.

Too many dreams and challenges have been put off to a later date. Now, without warning, that later date is all too well-defined and short. There's a lot to do and not much time to do it.

Just as if it were yesterday, I remember walking by a fellow worker, Al Thornwell, who was over 50. It was my 30th birthday. I was a bright young executive. Al whispered to someone, "I remember when I was his age. I wish I had his future rather than my past."

Now, my question to myself is whether or not that future has come and gone or whether it is still in progress. It's much nicer to think it is a work in progress.

I've gone in a heartbeat from being a young man with potential to an old man with memories but still with hopes for the future.

I had so much I wanted to do in this life. I still do. When I was a kid, I wanted to be a cowboy and a baseball player, and I wanted to go to Africa and to Australia and even just to sail a ship some place in any water that held islands.

As a teen, I just wanted to be popular.

College was a traumatic challenge. Getting through in four years seemed to me to be a remarkable achievement, since I didn't study and rarely went to class.

I was just happy to get out. School seemed like a waste of time at a time when there was time to waste. How I wish I could go back and study, even go to an Ivy League school and have a college record I could treasure. It passed me by.

Then, I needed a job. I had worked through school part-time for the Atlanta Braves. If you've got to work, you might as well work at a place that's fun. They put me in the public relations department. I became a public relations man. If they had put me part-time in the accounting department, I would have become an accountant. I had no problem finding myself, unlike many young people in the 1960s. Myself found me. I just showed up at the next spot on the chart and did whatever there was to do.

Don't get me wrong. I did whatever I was told and did it well. I ended up a vice president of the Atlanta Braves, and when Ted Turner bought the team and then also bought the Atlanta Hawks, I became a vice president of the Hawks, too. If Ted had bought a funeral home, I probably would have become a vice president of it, too — whatever I was told.

During this time I got married — not until I was 25, perilously old for marriage at that time in the South.

In the movies, the guys never just called the girl. They always sent them something clever, like roses every day for a week or something. It always worked for them. It never did for me. Until Susan came along.

Our meeting was right out of a movie.

As someone who worked for the local baseball team, I received lots of invitations to attend local conventions and meetings. One night, my friend Frank Spence with the local recreation department had asked me to drop by a hospitality suite he was hosting for a meeting of the Georgia Recreation and Park Society.

Not sure where the hospitality suite was, I mustered up enough nerve to knock on a door behind which a party was obviously going on. At that moment, it happened. A beautiful young woman, just like in the movies, swung open the door. She had a drink in her hand and was wearing "hot pants," the fashion vogue of the day. Hers were suede.

"Well, come on in," she said. "Who are you?" I told her my name was Bob Hope, and she didn't make a wise crack, which I really appreciated. She told me her name was Susan Snow. She was a real Braves fan, and during the evening she asked me a lot of questions about the team. I answered as enthusiastically as I could, trying to keep her attention away from her boyfriend.

When her boyfriend said he had always dreamed of playing on a big league field, I had my opening. I had keys to the new and exciting Atlanta-Fulton County Stadium. I could make that happen. Surely, that would impress her. So, I piled everyone into a caravan of cars, drove to the ballpark, opened the gates, and turned on the lights. I opened the clubhouses to get equipment, and we all played a baseball game. If she wasn't impressed, what else could I do?

It was hard to get a date with Susan, but I found I could get a date with her roommate Martha.

Over the next few weeks, I took Martha to the circus and invited Susan to go along. During the day before the night performance, I went through the trailers behind the old Atlanta civic auditorium where the circus was being held. I found Malakova, the star wire-walker, and we made a deal. I would come back to her trailer during intermission and bring two friends to meet her. Please, Malakova, pretend that we have known each other a long time and act like I'm a big deal.

She did. It seemed to go smoothly. I was impressed. I hoped Susan Snow was impressed, too.

Susan Snow is now Susan Hope. She's the mother of my two lovely daughters, Betsy and Clair, and a truly wonderful person. As it turned out, she thought I was making a fool of myself, but I was doing it for her. Somehow in all of that she understood. She is the best, and fate brought her to me.

Susan Hope (center), with daughters Betsy (left) and Clair

When I reached my 30s, brief twitches of aging entered my mind. I started jogging five miles every single day. This was quite an achievement for someone who had probably not jogged five miles in his entire life. I jogged painfully for seven years, and then, as quickly as I started,

I stopped. Hey, the thought of aging had passed. I didn't feel any older then than I did seven years earlier when I started jogging.

When I turned 40, I felt no panic or crisis. I began to notice in newspaper articles the age of people who were promoted to head big companies or who achieved great things, just to compare their age and accomplishments to mine.

The midlife crisis, I was certain, had passed me over. Many of my friends were divorcing their wives for younger women, frequently secretaries at the office. Some of the men just dropped out altogether. They'd vanish from the face of my earth overnight. I didn't have such trauma. I thought I felt fine.

Several months away from turning 16, my daughter Betsy was almost ready to begin driving. I needed a car. It made perfect sense that I should buy a car for Betsy, and as a favor to her, drive it until she reached driving age. I bought her a red convertible. Of course, a lot of people noted the connection to my turning 40, not understanding the good logic of the decision.

And, by the way, I moved to New York City.

Entering my 40s, I felt in a rut, doing the same job every day, living in the same city all my life. New York City was alluring. Had I lived in the time of ancient Greece, I would have wanted to hang out in Athens. In the 20th century, New York City was the place I needed to be. I was offered a job there and jumped at it. Susan, Betsy, and Clair reluctantly came along for my adventure.

Adventure filled many moments of my time in New York. I was a senior executive at Burson-Marsteller, the largest public relations firm in the city. I saw the famous people of business and entertainment every day.

Harold Burson, the chairman and founder of Burson-Marsteller, knew I enjoyed the big parties and events, as well as meeting famous people. He made sure some of his well-connected friends knew, too. Once, one of his friends told me to go by the restaurant "21" and ask for his party. I did. It was Katherine Hepburn's birthday party.

Another time Harold gave me two invitations to a tribute dinner for Broadway playwright Neil Simon, a favorite of my family. Susan and I were late for the black-tie affair. We entered the room and instantly got a feeling we weren't right at home. The place was full of celebrities and stars. As it turned out, it was a private party of close friends honoring Neil Simon. Susan and I were seated at a table with Jimmy Stewart and Tony Randall. Even though people kept asking us what our relationship was with Neil, we had a great time.

I was also on the board of directors of the Atlanta Braves during that time and received "director's seats" for Mets games, which made me feel real important and impressed my friends. It also meant I was on Ted Turner's "A" invitation list. When Ted came to New York, I'd get a call from his assistant, Dee Woods, to invite me to join him at various banquets and functions. I accepted. Ted always attracted stars and a crowd. That was fun.

My 40s was our decade of adventure.

It was also a decade of learning how tough change is and how there are things in life more important than prestige and security.

Susan never wanted to move to New York. She was well entrenched in the Atlanta community.

Betsy said she was willing to do whatever I wanted her to do.

Clair, on the other hand, simply refused to accept that we were moving at all. She not only didn't want to do it; in her way of thinking, it just wasn't going to happen.

I commuted from Atlanta for a year. We had a blast. Working in New York and returning to Atlanta for weekends gave me the best of all worlds. We kept our friends and home, and I got a chance to see what New York was like. When my family visited the Big Apple, we'd do everything from Broadway shows to street festivals, concerts, or the special events that take place in the city every day.

We then moved to Pelham, a very nice, tiny community just north of the city, and things got a little tougher.

After her first week at high school, Betsy informed me that she was miserable. She was president of the class — a big deal — in Atlanta. In New York, they didn't even know her.

Clair refused to speak to anyone. I'd ask her if she had made friends, and she'd tell me she had "only acquaintances."

Susan told me she was ready to move back South every day of the week for more than three years.

We finally managed to enjoy living in New York, even Clair, but Atlanta was our home and that's where we all eventually wanted to be.

Now, here I am in my 50s, back in Atlanta where I was born, and time is running out.

It cost a lot to get back South. I left all the financial perks of a big job. I haven't ridden in a limousine since. I don't look at my investment portfolio weekly to try to figure out how many millions I'll have when I retire. I just have to plan on not retiring. Continuing to work is not only a goal but a necessity.

I may seem old to some but I'm not close to being finished.

Marvin Runyon, who recently stepped down as Postmaster General of the U.S. Postal Service, is over 70. He took over the postal service when it was a financial disaster and left it operating at a profit. He is an amazing businessman. Our mutual friend, David Sable, had dinner with Marvin after he announced his resignation. Marvin told David he was looking for his next challenge. "Isn't he a little old for a new job?" I asked David. "Marvin doesn't think like other people," David said. "He thinks he'll live to be 100."

I want to live forever. However, pending that advancement in medicine, I want to make the most of the time I have left.

All of us come into the world in different places and in different situations. Some are rich, some are poor. Blacks have issues to face that whites will never know. Women are often ignored and slighted when they venture to do things that men take for granted. Some people are smarter than others. Some have more progressive and supportive parents. A few people have physical deformities. There are all kinds of wild cards in life.

Just as people win the lotto by chance, sometimes they achieve greatness by chance just by continuing to play the game.

Recently, my 101-year-old Aunt Rachel caused a stir in the old-folks home. After living alone all her life and never having so much as a date that anyone could recall, she now has a boyfriend — one who is, in fact, several years younger. They walk the halls holding hands and causing the grapevine to shake with gossip.

Somehow, that seems the way life should be.

THROW-AWAY PEOPLE

Several years ago I was sitting with my 85-year-old grandmother, "Mema," who had fallen and was recovering from a broken hip. For once, it was just the two of us. She told me something that day that I've never forgotten.

Mema was a delightful woman whose looks never seemed to change in more than forty years. It's a look that's now passé for older women. White-haired, heavyset but never seeming fat, with silky, cream-colored skin that wrinkled like Saran Wrap in places and wire-rimmed glasses, she looked just what I felt all grandmothers should look like. She wore simple cotton dresses, except on Sundays, when she would dress elegantly in black and put on enough makeup to make her cheeks turn pink.

With four daughters, a son, and a total number of grandchildren and great grandchildren in the forties — a number that seemed to change weekly, she was matriarch of a large clan and had rightful claim to the name Mema. That's the only name I ever heard her called.

On Christmas Eve, the entire family would gather and celebrate, including uncles, aunts, nieces, nephews, and cousins from Georgia, Alabama, and as far away as Michigan. Few of us had seen each other in the year leading up to the event, but all of us had seen Mema several times.

She was always upbeat and happy. She always had a kind word.

Her husband abandoned her and their five children long before I was born. She worked and raised them by herself.

After Mema broke her hip, I had put off going to see her for a few days. She had always seemed so self-sufficient and had lived alone my entire life. And we'd never had anything that resembled a heart-to-heart conversation. In 1922, Willa Cather wrote a line that might sum up our relationship, "The dead might as well try to speak to the living as the old to the young." I loved my grandmother, but a nice chat was never part of our time together.

As I sat on the Victorian sofa in Mema's living room and began talking, it quickly became obvious that I was really there to listen.

She told me how much she loved me and how much it meant to her that Susan and I had a happy family. Her treatment from my grandfather had obviously not been good. Then, she said the thing that I would always remember. She talked about growing old.

"Sometimes I'm tired and don't want to get up in the morning," she said. "I think about living alone and about how it really might not matter if I got up and got dressed and fixed a full breakfast, but then I do it. You are alive as long as you are getting up each day and doing things. When you start backing off, you are dying."

"Wow," I thought. Since that day, I've never quite been able to sleep late. I just get up and get going each day. Her words stuck.

I've been intrigued and also annoyed for years at how some young people (who will, by the way, grow old too if they are lucky) give little credit to the experience and wisdom of their older folks.

When I worked at the Coca-Cola Company several years ago, my boss was a 52-year-old executive named Bruce Gilbert. Bruce looked the part of an over-50 executive. While some of his counterparts worked to stay trim, dyed their hair, or even had hairpieces, Bruce seemed at peace being a little overweight and bald. He had been head of marketing and advertising at Coke in what was regarded as the company's glory days.

Bruce was responsible for a lot of the work that made Coke the leader

GREATER LATE THAN NEVER

in advertising creativity. He was the first to use popular singing groups in radio advertising. During his watch, Coke became the "Real Thing" and great TV ads were created such as the one with a mass of young people from all nations on a hillside singing "I'd Like To Teach the World To Sing."

I worked for Coke for two years. It was the first time I witnessed what corporate America views as a necessary evil — moving veteran senior employees aside to make room for the young bucks.

I thought Bruce Gilbert was terrific, a great man and wonderful example of achievement. However, as younger and fiercer MBAs entered the Coca-Cola Company, they seemed to totally discount the wisdom as well as the contributions of such people as Bruce.

Whatever Bruce was assigned to do while I worked at Coke was done far better than the young Turks might have done. He orchestrated the "Great Get-together," an incredible convention of Coca-Cola bottlers from throughout the United States. There were red Coca-Cola banners on every light pole in San Francisco. Billboards were everywhere. Huge parties took place, with dancers, bands, and more food than I had ever seen. Everything went like clockwork.

While I was at Coke, nobody, other than Bruce, ever suggested that the Olympics might be used in a major way in marketing, and his bosses basically told him to shut up and not push something as stupid as the Olympics being anything particularly special for Coke. At that time, many of the people at Coke felt the money spent on the Olympics could be used in better ways. "Just give me the money we spend on the Olympics and let me show you what I could do with it" was a common phrase.

Bruce showed class in everything he did. Young executives coming on the scene sometimes seemed to have anything but class, displaying a unique talent for making a lot of noise and bragging on themselves.

A brash, young executive from Pepsi named Sergio Zyman became head of marketing for Coke's U.S. operations. It seemed from the start that his attitude was simple: Everything Pepsi did was right; everything Coke did was wrong.

By the business standards of most observers, Sergio would measure up as a real dynamo. He was intense and determined to change the ways of a company that, at the time, Ted Turner had described to me as a "stale old company with a stale old product and stale old people." However, I viewed him primarily as a threat to a good man, Bruce Gilbert, and others like Bruce who had helped build a great company.

One of his first moves was to change the annual Coca-Cola calendars that had been produced for fifty years. You've seen these calendars. They are treasures for collectors of Coca-Cola memorabilia. Tiny mom-and-pop stores across America had nails on walls or doors where the Coca-Cola calendars were placed in honored spots each year.

When Sergio, who was then in his early 30s, saw the calendar that had been printed for the upcoming year, he tore one up, threw it down, and stomped on it.

He ordered that it be redone in a new poster format, wasting hundreds of thousands of dollars.

So, new calendars were printed, sent out, and then sent back by customers of Coke who couldn't understand why something simple, effective, and dear to them didn't fit in the traditional spot reserved for it. It was a mystery, but to Sergio it was a sign of progress. Anything old was bad. Only new things and new ideas were good.

Sergio led the charge for "new thinking" at Coke. A typical TV commercial cost Coke about $100,000 to produce. Sergio spent $500,000 to produce a commercial for Christmas. He filmed the commercial at Disneyland during the heat of mid-summer. Disneyland was transformed into a winter wonderland with manufactured snow. When the commercial was previewed to Coke executives, it looked like an alpine village. However, somehow, someone forgot to put in the Disney characters or any other reference that would give you any idea that hundreds of thousands of dollars had been spent to make a hot place look like a cold place. They could have just gone to a cold place to film it and saved a lot of money. That's progress?

In spite of making some mistakes, Sergio was bright and was considered the new breed of executive, and the new breed seemed to have no time or respect for the old breed that had gotten Coke to its present position. Any sign of respect for the heritage of the company was viewed as resting on past laurels, an attitude that wasn't to be tolerated.

Bruce Gilbert was moved aside, demoted, stripped of his vice presidency, and finally retired.

It seemed to me at the time, in fact, that most Coke executives were cast aside after they turned 50 unless they happened to be chairman of the board or president. The very top held strong. The rest, it seemed, were judged and placed in a "no-longer-needed" category.

The same thing happened to Marc Hamburger, the 50-year-old former vice president of worldwide marketing at Coke. He was an outstanding thinker, one of the best I've seen.

One thing that has impressed me about a few business leaders I've known is their ability to zero right in on a subject and analyze it in its most basic terms. When Wayne Huizenga (another older executive) was building Blockbuster, he was a client of mine. I'd explain something that seemed complex to me. He'd say, what you are saying is "1, 2, 3," breaking it down to its most simple terms. Ted Turner could do that, too. He'd keep things very simple. Marc had the same knack.

Marc was put in charge of planning the 1996 Olympics for Coke, the biggest marketing expenditure in the history of the company. Marc hired our firm to work with him on his plan. We came up with such bold new ideas as Coca-Cola Olympic City, a theme park that would be built in downtown Atlanta. We invented the Coca-Cola Olympic Pin Trading Society, producing literally millions of collector pins — a huge success. We painted giant Coke bottles on walls in downtown Atlanta, even having the bottle declared a state symbol so we wouldn't have to work with the normal restrictions that ruled the size of outdoor advertisements.

Marc was brilliant.

Once the planning was done and the budgets approved, Doug Ivester, then president of the Coca-Cola Company, made a typical corporate change. He replaced age with youth. He brought in a younger executive to do the work. Marc was sent out to corporate pasture. The Olympics went great for Coke, and the new, young executive got the credit. Without a doubt, he did a good job. But what he did was what Marc Hamburger had planned and gotten approved. Marc wasn't around for the glory.

Age once again became the enemy in a corporate world that wants everyone to be young.

This attitude about anyone over age 50 holds true not just at Coke. It's a disease in most American institutions. Age is not respected, but discarded.

Sergio, by the way, continued to charge ahead in his effort to change the Coca-Cola world, finally convincing Coke that its primary product didn't taste good enough to beat Pepsi. So Coke changed its formula to taste more like Pepsi.

New Coke didn't work.

That was Sergio's last hurrah. He was gone from the scene soon after that.

Several years later Sergio was brought back by Coke to head its marketing again. This time he was older and wiser, nearly 50 himself. This time the great Coca-Cola trademark didn't seem so desperately in need of change. He built a stronger company by bringing back the old bottle shape and by using the advertising campaign of "Always Coca-Cola," a theme used first in the 1930s. He presented Coca-Cola as a strong, reliable, and honest friend, and the product has flourished.

But, as the cycle continued, young executives at Coke attacked Sergio's approach as being stale, not hip or hot enough to charm and attract teenagers of today. Sergio, the younger ones said, lost touch. He became too old.

The scouts went out looking for the newer and younger version. Sergio resigned earlier this year.

As the saying goes: things change, but things never change.

In a world where people now live to be 80 or 90, it is hard to believe people over 50 are really on their way out — both out of their careers and out of life. Too many people are being put out to pasture when they have both wonderful knowledge and immense ability.

It seems a great waste. What happens in a world where the wisdom gained from age is not used or appreciated?

The answer can't be good.

It doesn't just happen at Coke. Recently a friend called. He had worked at Eastman Kodak for twenty-three years. The company had just announced a bad-earnings performance. Hundreds of people would be dropped from the payroll in an attempt to right the ship. I asked whether he was worried. "Of course I am," he answered. "I'm a 50-year-old, white male, and no company feels it needs one of those anymore. I'm just hanging on and waiting for the ax to fall."

I don't understand an attitude that emerged in my generation. Regardless of health or mental state, people were expected to retire when they reached 60, or at the very least, by 65. If they had enough money to retire before reaching those ages, they wanted to stop working and start easing up on life anytime after 50.

I have friends who talk in their 40s about wanting to retire in their 50s. It sounds nice when they say it. But retire to what? What do they intend to do every day when they get up in the morning? I can't imagine it.

People in the United States who are over age 50 have 42 percent more disposable income than the average person. They have the capacity to do a lot of wonderful things with their lives.

By 2025, more than 40 percent of all adults will be over age 50. That's a lot of folks to throw away and ignore. If they would all get out and do something, the results could be staggering.

A lot of people retire from their jobs and then die soon afterward. When someone retires, they seem to get older a lot quicker. I have new respect for people who want to keep going with their lives.

Baseball legend Satchel Paige said a lot of things that people love to quote. News reporters and ballplayers alike would crowd into the dugout to hear his colorful remarks and benefit from his wisdom. In my early days of working for the Atlanta Braves, we signed Satchel one season as a coach, not really to coach players but to give him enough time on our big league roster to qualify for the big league pension plan. That was in 1967, and he was in his 60s. Without any pressing duties to instruct on the field, he had plenty of time to instruct from his bench in the bullpen.

All of us became acquainted with his sayings, such as, "Don't look back because someone may be catching up with you," or "Don't eat meat because it angries up the blood."

One of my favorites was, "Getting old is mind over matter; if you don't mind, it don't matter."

Satchel Paige

Satchel believed in that. He pitched until he was 50.

In today's world, that sounds right. It really doesn't matter how old you are. If you want to do something, do it. Don't spend years relaxing as you grow older. You'll be totally relaxed forever once you die.

Take a look at these facts from the U.S. Census Bureau and *Successful Aging* by Drs. John Rowe and Robert Kahn:

- While the average person who was born in 1900 could expect to live to age 47, anyone born today in the United States can expect to live to 76.

- One in nine baby boomers will live late into their 90s.

- One in twenty-six will live to be 100. In 1940, there were 3,700 people in the United States 100 or older. Today, there are 61,000. By 2030, when people age 50 today will be a mere 82, there will be more than one million centenarians in America. In short, 50 may really be middle age.

- And, only 5 percent of people over age 65 live in nursing homes. So most people will need something challenging to do.

- Guys need to push harder, faster. Four out of five 100-year-olds are women.

If you don't keep active and challenged after turning 50, you could have a long, boring stretch ahead.

"I believe that man will not merely endure; he will prevail. He is immortal, not because he alone among creatures has an inexhaustible voice, but because he has a soul, a spirit capable of compassion and sacrifice and endurance."

— William Faulkner

BUILDING UP FOR A SECOND WIND

There is a saying that the most segregated time in America is on Sunday morning at 11 A.M. when church services are being held. When blacks moved in to the old Kirkwood neighborhood of Atlanta thirty years ago, the members of the Kirkwood United Methodist Church decided to move en masse and form St. Timothy United Methodist Church in Stone Mountain, reaching out farther into the suburbs and into an area where only white people lived at the time. My family now attends this 600 member church.

I didn't go to Kirkwood and wasn't involved in the early days of St. Timothy. I imagine I know what the feelings were. When the skin of new members starts changing colors, the spoken word within the congregation is to reach out and show that all people are welcome in the fellowship. The unspoken word is discomfort, and discomfort tends to stifle growth and cause many old members to leave.

That's what is happening again at St. Timothy. The neighborhood around the church is transitioning from white to black. Membership is falling, contributions are fading.

In the United Methodist church, there is what is called the itinerate preacher system. That means that preachers move randomly from one church to another every few years, based on what the high-ranking officials of the church think is best for the individual local church.

Typically, because St. Timothy is a mid-sized church in the Atlanta suburbs, it would get dynamic young preachers who would later go on to become the ministers of the largest churches in the state and, in most cases, the leaders in the overall denomination.

Now, however, because of the changes in membership and funding at the church, St. Timothy would be assigned an older minister. His name was Renfroe Watson, and he made the plight of being over 50 hit home hard.

Granted, I'm over 50, but that doesn't mean I wasn't stunned when I heard the news.

I was particularly dismayed because Renfroe was replacing a bright, extremely committed minister who had formed a movement to clean up local parks, work with local merchants to rebuild their declining businesses, and put on events to pull together the diverse cultures in the Stone Mountain community. Our young minister was making real progress, and the bishop decided to put him behind a desk as a district superintendent.

My first thought was that this new man must not be any good or he wouldn't still be preaching in a middle-of-the-pack church. Why hadn't he graduated to some desk job like district superintendent or even bishop?

So, here comes Renfroe Watson — all five-foot-five of him.

I wasn't prepared for what I saw.

First, he wasn't much older than I am. That in itself is a solid dose of reality. I was expecting something resembling a codger, for some reason.

Second, he had more energy and pure enthusiasm than any of the previous ministers we'd had at the church, a real dynamo.

And, finally, he is an excellent storyteller.

One story seemed enormously appropriate at the time, and it introduces this chapter of the book quite well.

Renfroe Watson

Renfroe was on the track team in high school. He ran the half-mile, which he figured must be the most difficult distance because everyone running the other races didn't look nearly as tired as he felt.

"I can remember the most important race I ever ran," Renfroe began.

"It was against a runner from a rival school who had always beaten me in the past."

The half-mile race is a difficult one, he explained, because the entire distance is run nearly at full speed. The theory is to hold back just a little during the first half of the race, one full lap around the track. Then, run as fast as you possibly can for the remainder.

Renfroe decided to take off, run the first lap at full speed, build a lead, and then hope he could hold it the rest of the way.

He led the runners for the first lap.

"Suddenly, I was out of breath, something was wrong," he said. "As hard as a tried, I couldn't make my legs move. I could hear the runners behind me getting closer, but I couldn't do anything about it. They were catching up, and I felt like I was dying. I just couldn't do it."

Then, he said, something amazing happened.

"Something overcame my body, and I took off running. I could breathe easy. Every step was easy. I felt better than I had in the beginning of the race. Effortlessly, I went on to win."

He then went to his coach and excitedly told him about his miracle. When he was explaining the spirit that had leaped into his body and taken over, the coach responded, "Son, don't you know what that was? That was your second wind. When you think you've gone as hard and far as you possibly can, your second wind kicks in."

HAROLD BURSON

Burson-Marsteller owned Cohn & Wolfe, the public relations firm I had helped build in Atlanta. The largest firm in the business, Burson-Marsteller was about to go through some major changes at its headquarters. The founder, Harold Burson, was over 65, and it was time for a change in senior management. Jim Dowling, whom he had mentored for years, would be named the new chief executive officer. Harold was to semiretire. I was asked to go to New York to work with the new management team.

Harold's title changed to chairman emeritus, a recognition of his-building the worldwide company. It amazed me how such a kind man who never raised his voice could build the world's largest company in anything.

He had reached his pinnacle in corporate life, and it was time for him to wind down.

That didn't last very long.

While I was in New York, I would take the 6:40 A.M. train from my home in little Pelham to Grand Central Station. It was the way to beat the rush. That meant I was in the office by 7:30. The only other person there was Harold.

One night, Harold and I attended a banquet. Someone asked Harold if he still came to work every day. I blurted out the answer for him, noting that he was in the office at 7:30 every morning when I arrived.

Harold snapped back that I arrived at the office at 7:30. He was there each morning before 7 A.M.

Harold Burson

Today, ten years later, Harold is 77 years old and still in the office each morning at seven. His title of chairman emeritus has been upgraded back to chairman, and he is as active as ever in the company he founded.

One of the stories Harold likes to tell is about Baseball Hall of Fame player Ty Cobb. When Cobb was 77, a sportswriter asked him how he thought he would hit in the modern game of baseball, now that so many changes have taken place.

"I think I would probably hit about .290," Cobb answers. (Cobb's batting average was .360.)

"Only .290?" the sportswriter questioned.

"Well, you have to remember I'm 77 years old," Cobb says.

Harold at 77 is still, in his way of thinking, well capable of hitting .290, which is better than most.

RALPH WALDO EMERSON JONES

In the early 1970s, the Braves had a young outfielder named Ralph Garr. We called him the "Road Runner." He would swing at any pitch and scatter hits to all fields. No player was more exciting to watch. He led the National League in hitting in 1971. That prompted me to call his college baseball coach, R. W. E. Jones, to find out more about Ralph.

I called Grambling State University and asked for Coach Jones. The operator connected me to an extension where someone answered "president's residence." When I explained I had the wrong number, the man on the other end of the phone introduced himself. "I'm Ralph Waldo Emerson Jones, the president of Grambling and the baseball coach."

So I was introduced to a man I would like to be, probably the most intriguing and delightful personality I've ever met.

Dr. R. W. E. Jones retired in 1977 after fifty-one years at Grambling State University, a predominantly black college in Grambling, Louisiana. He joined the faculty of Grambling in 1925 when it was called the Louisiana Negro Normal and Industrial Institute and had only 120 students. No one seems to know exactly how old he was when he retired, but when he came to the school as a math teacher, he already had his bachelor's degree from Southern University, his master's from Columbia University, and his doctorate from Louisiana Tech. He was somewhere in the neighborhood of 80 years old when he quit. Thank goodness for the second wind.

Grambling didn't just lose a college president and baseball coach when Dr. Jones stepped down, it also lost its band director, a math professor, and a legend. He did it all.

He started the baseball program at Grambling when other black schools had no teams, and white schools wouldn't play them. The first few seasons, the team played exhibitions against professional Negro League teams with such famous players as Satchel Paige, Josh Gibson, and Cool Papa Bell, who are now in the National Baseball Hall of Fame.

He started the football team, the basketball team, and the band. He hired legendary football coach Eddie Robinson, who was inducted into the College Football Hall of Fame in 1997. The school had one of the most successful women's basketball teams in the country prior to World War II when most colleges didn't have women's sports teams.

Over the years, he found ways to keep the school going as it struggled from being a group of wooden buildings and seventeen teachers to a major center of academics having 10,000 students and a sprawling campus.

"I have the greatest job in the world," President/Coach Jones told me when I called. "As baseball coach, I work for Eddie Robinson, our football coach and athletic director. He approves my budget. However, as president of Grambling, I approve his budget. We seem to be able to get things done."

Coach Jones had a record of 722 wins and only 179 losses. His teams produced such big leaguers as Ralph Garr and former New York Mets stars Tommie Agee and Cleon Jones. But he was far more than a coach.

"He was absolutely the nicest human being I ever met in my life," Garr remembers. "I'm not much for talking about giving black people special breaks, but he did more for young black people than anyone.

"It's really tough to explain what he meant to his athletes," Garr continues. "He raised us as a family and loved everybody. He was our coach, and he made us work hard. We had one of the most outstanding college baseball programs in the country. But he was also our school's president. The priority for him was that we go to class and graduate. He made sure we did that. I bet more players who played on his teams graduated than at any other school in the country.

"When I was in high school, people thought I was too little to play baseball," Ralph Garr notes. "One day, Coach Jones stopped me on the street and said, 'You're name's Ralph, right?' I told him it was. 'My name's Ralph, too. You must be a decent person.'"

Garr got a baseball scholarship to Grambling but he got far more. R. W. E. Jones sent him to the dentist to have his teeth fixed, made sure he had a summer job, and even gave him a little extra money along the way when he needed it.

"There's not a list long enough for me to tell you the nice things I saw him do for people," Garr says. "He had the respect of everybody and helped with everything. He knew how to handle human beings and knew how to help you help yourself."

For Grambling's 80th anniversary in 1981, the school newspaper printed a story written in tribute to Dr. Ralph Waldo Emerson Jones. It ended, "Dr. Jones, now retired, is a living example of the exceedingly rare fact that sometimes it can all be put together. How else, located in relative isolation, in academics, sports, drama, humanities and community relations, would Grambling be today one of America's foremost landmark institutions?"

TOMMY BARNES

Last summer I made a speech to the Albany, Georgia, Sports Hall of Fame. I did it as a favor to Dee Matthews, who is a good friend and ranks with Susan as one of the most avid University of Georgia sports fans in existence. My company's women's baseball team, the Silver Bullets, was playing fifteen games in Albany during the summer. Dee originally wanted Phil Niekro to make the speech. When Phil wasn't available, she asked me instead. I didn't mind being a pinch hitter. A party for the invitees was held the night before at a local country club, with a golf outing planned for the next day.

One of the people I met that night was a old-time member of the Georgia Sports Hall of Fame. His name was Tommy Barnes, a golfer. He was 81 years old. I was somewhat surprised he stayed until the end of the party. I was also surprised when they told me he would be my golf partner the next day. I knew I wasn't much of a golfer, but an 81-

year-old partner? Surely, somebody was playing a joke on me.

Tommy Barnes shot seventy-two the next day, better by far than anyone else in the group.

He told me his story. He was an outstanding young golfer and a friend
of golf legend Bobby Jones. However, when he turned 60, he started to
slow down.

Tommy Barnes in 1958

Tommy had started playing the game at age 6 and won his first tournament at 9. At age 15, Tommy finished second in the City Amateur
Championship. He went on to play golf for Georgia Tech and has won
more than eighty golf tournaments in his lifetime.

"I backed off in 1955," he recalled. "I had won the Southern Amateur
Championship in 1947 and 1949, and I played in the Masters in 1950.
However, I had a family, and I needed to get serious and make some
money."

Tommy had been working in the real estate department of Pure Oil
Company. He decided to either become a professional golfer or to go
into real estate. He took the real estate route.

Tommy continued to play, although not as seriously as he once did. However, the game remained his passion and made him a legend when most other athletes had long since quit. At age 73, he broke Bobby Jones's 67-year-old course record at Jones's home course, Atlanta's East Lake Country Club. Tommy shot 62 — 11 strokes under his age.

"Furman Bisher (a long-time *Atlanta Journal* columnist) submitted it to the Guinness Book of World Records," Tommy recalled. "He got a report back that it wasn't a record because two different 83-year-old golfers had shot rounds of 70 — 13 strokes under their age." Barnes is likely to break those records, too.

At 81, his handicap is the highest it's ever been, a six. He recently shot 69 in a tournament. "I had an easy shot for a birdie on the 18th hole," he laughed, "but I choked."

Tommy Barnes in 1998

Six years ago, Tommy passed the test to get his real estate license. Before that, he made his living by owning gasoline stations and speculating in land. At age 75, he started brokering land, too. He just completed a deal for a 300-acre resort with the same company that developed Grand Cypress Resort in Orlando.

His latest project is the development and marketing of a line of "Tommy Barnes" golf clubs and clothing for senior, women, and children golfers.

What's next for Tommy Barnes?

"I'm hoping for a pro tour for golfers 80 and over," he smiled. "And my businesses will keep me busy.

"Golf has been good for me. I meet great people from all over the world, and I really enjoy the sport. I get my most enjoyment now showing other people how to improve their golf. It's a hard game to play. And even though it can be frustrating to work with a beginner, I have a lot of patience.

"I just completed a physical exam," he continued. "My blood pressure was 130 over 70, and the doctor asked me what kind of diet I was on because I had the lowest cholesterol he'd ever seen. They told me I'll get going strong at 100.

"I plan to keep playing and to break 100 in golf at age 100," he said.

— — — — —

Tommy Barnes, Ralph Waldo Emerson Jones, and Harold Burson all have life's second wind. Tommy is shooting in the 70s and loving it, while Harold is holding onto his .290 average. Ralph Jones batted a thousand.

Author James Michener told a story about an apple orchard on his foster mother's farm when he was growing up in Pennsylvania. The trees were old and dying. They had been there for years and had stopped producing fruit or even leaves.

An old man was hired to chop them down. Instead, the old man took some big, rusty nails and drove them into the base of the trees. Within days, the trees were turning green again and continued to produce fruit for years.

The old man told young Jim Michener, "Sometimes it just takes a jolt to make something realize what it can still do."

THE SECRETS OF STAYING YOUNG

It's not hard to find advice on how to keep youthful. I found literally hundreds of books on how to keep from growing old: *Stop Aging Now*, *The Anti-Aging Bible*, Dr. *Mollen's Anti-Aging Diet*, or try alternative medicine and *Stay Young the Melatonin Way*.

However, the aging body and the aging mind are two different things, and no one has captured the real secret. The secret is in making the most of growing old.

"This [staying young] has been the quest that people have had throughout the history of civilization, long before the fountain of youth," says Dr. Gene Cohen, director of the Center on Aging, Health and Humanities at George Washington University. "People have tried some pretty wild things."

In the middle ages, the blood of young men was taken and used to replace the blood of old men to bring back their youth.

In most cases, aging is viewed as a disease, as if enough research will find a cure.

A recent headline in *Time* magazine rang loud, "The Immortality Enzyme." The subhead read, "A newly discovered gene may help scientists combat cancer and ailments linked with age."

The story explains that each time a cell divides, it sheds part of its structure. That's how the body grows old. By rebuilding something called "telomeres," the body could possibly stop getting old.

While doctors are busy finding ways to prolong life for people who can't figure out what to do on a rainy day, the rest of us are stuck with figuring out what to do with the time we have.

"I've seen thousands of older people, and I've come to the conclusion that there are really just three factors that keep someone going and productive in old age," says Larry Minnix, the president of Emory University's Wesley Woods Center in Atlanta, which includes a geriatrics division. Minnix has been studying the aging process at Emory for twenty-five years.

"First, there is the issue of genetics. Some people are just physically stronger and their bodies stay healthier for a longer time. In most cases, if a person is healthy in their early life, they stay healthy later on.

"Second is attitude. Some people just keep a good attitude no matter what happens. Intimacy has something to do with it. If people are close to others, their attitudes tend to be more positive. And there are some people who complain about a hangnail while some don't make a big deal out of having cancer. If a person has a sour personality early in life, that same person will probably have one late, too.

"Third is faith and hope and a belief in something beyond this life. That doesn't necessarily mean a secular belief. It can just be a feeling about a higher purpose. The people who see purpose in their lives tend to keep going."

Wesley Woods has a banquet each year to honor "Heroes, Saints and Legends" — people who do remarkable things after age 70. "We honor three or four every year, and each is a remarkable story," he notes.

Physical aging at this point can't be reversed. Another Emory aging expert, Dr. Carl Hug, says the body is challenged every day to replace its cells and revitalize itself over and over again. At some point in time, it becomes fragile and something happens that it can't overcome.

Vitamins can help, but they don't make you younger, just healthier.

The answer may just be in the way people look at their lives.

In his book *Ageless Body, Timeless Mind,* Dr. Deepak Chopra writes, "The decline in vigor in old age is largely the result of people expecting to decline. Long before you get old, you can prevent such losses by consciously programming your mind to remain youthful, using the power of your intention."

After watching and talking to an assortment of people in researching this book, I've come up with the common traits that the ever-young seem to possess:

1. Use it or lose it. Dr. Hug says growing old physically is the process of the body losing its ability to regenerate itself. If you stop doing something, the body may lose its ability to do it. Stop working out, you get weaker. Stop running, you can't run as far. Get out of shape, it gets harder to get back into shape. So, the most important rule is to keep on doing what you do. Don't back off and don't give your body a chance to quit. Stay in shape and keep going full-speed ahead.

2. Go to the doctor. Dr. Hug says an aging body is like an old car. You've got to take care of it and fix every problem to keep it running smooth.

3. Be excited. Eddie Mathews played third base for the Milwaukee Braves teams that won the National League Championship in 1956, 1957, and 1958 and the World Series in 1957. I got to know Eddie when he was manager of the Braves in 1973 and 1974. The Braves had a series of very poor-performing teams but also had Hank Aaron chasing Babe Ruth's all-time home run record. Eddie got all he could get out of those teams, and his 1974 team, in fact, finished second.

Eddie was rough around the edges. He had a quick temper, and he drank too much. I stopped going out to have a drink with him in spring training after bar brawls seemed to break out everywhere we went. Eddie lost his job as Braves manager not because he didn't have the team winning enough games, but because his drinking got out of hand. When he had the team bus stop so that he could run in a liquor store and buy some beer, the word got back to the front office. It was the last straw.

However, Eddie was a winner. His secret was simple. He'd tell the team that they had to love what they were doing. He wanted them to have a great time. He told how the 1957 Braves had tricycles in the clubhouse and would have tricycle races each day when they got to the ballpark.

The secret, he said, was to look forward to getting up every morning. That philosophy seems right for staying young.

In a Presbyterian Church survey, 85 percent of the church members said they were very satisfied with their lives, but only 11 percent said they were excited about their lives. Do something that will make your life exciting.

I'm reminded of a biography written about Joe Namath. Its title was, appropriately, *I Can't Wait Until Tomorrow, I Get Better Looking Every Day.*

4. **Believe in something.** Bill Saum, our former minister at New York's Pelham Presbyterian Church, graduated from Harvard. He was a scruffy, frail-looking, glasses-wearing character in his 50s, bald on top with light brown hair frazzling over his ears. Nothing about him would lead you to believe he would be a great speaker. But what he had to say was captivating.

When the time came for his 25th reunion at Harvard, he was asked to speak to the graduates — most were successful businessmen and even heads of big companies.

The point of his talk was simple. All the graduates had gone to Harvard in the 1960s, at a time when they were noted for their liberal convictions and determination to remedy the problems of the world. Now, twenty-five years later, they had totally changed.

"Why is it that people dream of doing great things and changing the world into a better place when they are in college and have no money or power, but then when they get money and power and are older, they don't do anything?" He was troubled by the question, and the audience was troubled that it had no answer. Most had fallen into the routine of their own lives and were basically serving their time on earth. They were the ones who could do something. They weren't doing it.

People who speed up in the later years all seem to have a passion for something they are doing, something they feel is more important than the ordinary things in daily life.

5. **Be serious about life.** The whole concept of retirement seems to be built around the idea that someone can quit work and piddle the remainder of his or her life. That isn't conducive to a long and productive life. Many simple things can be turned into something remarkable if one is willing to take himself seriously. We have a friend, Pearl Sandow, who is well into her 90s. She was the most remarkable fan of the Atlanta Braves. She was such a great fan that a statue of her now stands in the Baseball Hall of Fame. The Braves didn't move to Atlanta until Pearl was over 60. She attended 1,889 consecutive Braves' home games before a broken shoulder at age 90 forced her to miss one. Her consecutive game record is the fan counterpart of Cal Ripkin's. She took herself seriously as a baseball fan and became a star by doing so.

6. **Do it now.** When I was young, it was easy to put things off. After working several years with Ted Turner, I realized that he wasn't particularly smarter than the rest of us. His ideas weren't that much better than ideas others had. He just went and did things. He never put anything off to a later date.

Yes, life spans are expanding. But you can't take for granted that there will always be "a later date." Let me take a moment to give one sobering warning from Dr. Hug:

"In the past, doctors have tended to be optimistic with patients, presenting to them the best case of what can happen after a particular procedure. With the population growing older and remaining healthy longer, doctors are frequently being called on to operate on older patients. In these cases, there are a variety of options to discuss and explain to the patients. Older people have decreased reserves. They recover much slower than younger patients, and there is not much margin for error. They need to understand what they are facing and that there are options.

"I use the example of grandma who is 80," he continues. "She lives alone and keeps her own apartment, cooks, walks every day, and someone takes her to church. Suddenly, one day, she comes down with coronary artery disease. An operation could bring her back to normal or it might leave her debilitated. There is a risk. And she has to decide whether or not, at her age, she wants to take that risk. By not having an operation, she will be restricted in what she can do but will continue to have control of her functions. If the operation doesn't work, she needs to understand the consequences."

Dr. Carl Hug

At age 61, Dr. Hug is a good example himself of seizing the moment to do something important. He is about to step down as the Director of Cardiothoracic Anesthesiology at Emory University Hospital. Retirement for him means cutting back his time with patients to about 40 percent while still traveling the globe to give seminars as the world's renowned expert on the use of opoids — strong painkillers for the dying or gravely ill.

"There are very sensitive ethical questions that doctors must face in treatment of older people today," he continues. "I've always had an interest in ethics. I'm not trained in the area, but I intend to get up to speed and learn all I can. It is important that doctors approach healthy, older people in the right way when they discuss options. I want to use my retirement to contribute in this area."

You don't know how much time you have left. Don't put things off. If we are to keep young and vibrant, we need to do the things we dream of doing and do them now.

7. Ignore defeats.

The ends on our high school football team would always start the season by slamming their fists on the ground whenever they dropped a pass. The coach would tell them over and over to forget the mistake. The point was simple. It does no good to dwell on a mistake or defeat. Get it out of your mind and go on to the next task.

Ted Turner had the best attitude about failure. He'd boast that failure wasn't final. One of the great things about living in America, he'd say, was that no one killed you if you failed when you tried something.

When you venture into anything that is really an adventure, failure is a possibility. If you fail, you can get right up and go again.

One thing that seems to go with getting older is fear of trying anything new. I have friends who hate what they are doing but won't change. They would rather suffer than risk not having money stashed away for retirement. Somehow, this seems crazy. Keep trying to do things that are inspiring and new. Don't fear failure.

8. Forget your age.

As the saying goes, "Age is only important if you are a cheese." Several years ago, I was making a speech in Miami, Florida, on whether or not Miami would be a good spot for a major league baseball team. I had worked with Charlotte to get the Hornets for the NBA and then with Ottawa when it went after the Senators team in the National Hockey League.

Don Smiley, assistant to Wayne Huizenga, the chairman of Blockbuster Video, was in the audience. Wayne had started Blockbuster just three years earlier, and it was booming into the largest video rental chain in the world. Smiley said Wayne wanted to be the person to go after a team for Miami.

Over the next few months, I got to know Wayne very well. He was 53 years old when I met him and showed no signs of letting up. His father, Harry, was in his 80s and came to most of the meetings we had.

Blockbuster was not Wayne's first business success. He was one of the founders of Waste Management Corp., the largest waste collection company in the world. Wayne bought and started businesses with a passion.

Since I've met Wayne, he sold Blockbuster to Viacom. He then bought Republic Waste and changed its name to Republic Industries. He bought the Miami Dolphins of the NFL and the Florida Panthers of the NHL. He bought the Boca Club resort and several Marriott hotels.

Wayne is now 60, and he just keeps on going. He shows no signs of letting up. Age seems of no concern to him. He is ageless.

$9.$ **Make a difference.** It probably isn't necessary to feel that you are special, but it seems like it would be a shame if someone who could stand out among the nearly six billion people on earth doesn't try to do it. Jimmy Carter was OK as a president but has been remarkable as a former president. He has made a difference by writing inspirational books, working on Habitat for Humanity, and representing the United States in delicate negotiations all over the world.

When everything else is the same, it is nice to think you are doing something that makes the world a little better.

I once heard someone ask Ted Turner if he really thought it was any of his business to tamper in areas of global sensitivity. Ted had started the Goodwill Games with the hope that the sports event would somehow contribute to the fall of the Iron Curtain, and he created the Better World Society to help bring peace to the world, eliminate hunger, and clean up the environment.

"Don't get me wrong," he answered. "I know what I am. I'm a broadcaster. I own TV networks. That's how I make a living. World peace? World peace is my hobby. I think other people should try having the same hobby."

Paul Perconti, the chief executive officer of Thornton Oil Corporation, says the secret to a long life is being comfortable with your spot in life. If you aren't in the right spot, change it, he says. You've got to have a reason to live.

10. Chase a dream. Ray Kroc founded McDonald's when he was 50. When he was in his 70s, he bought the San Diego Padres baseball team.

One night I was attending the Baseball Winter Meetings banquet in Honolulu, Hawaii. I worked for the Braves then. The team was usually in last place, but we had bigger and wilder promotions than any other team. We were always looking forward to the next season, and we always expected to win.

I sat at the same table with Ray Kroc. As we were talking about the Braves' struggle, the team was presented with the award for having the best minor league system in baseball. That meant the young players for the Braves were regarded as the best in the game.

Mr. Kroc seemed very happy to be sitting with a losing team. He offered us his words of advice: "It's a hell of a lot more fun chasing it than it is when you finally catch it," he said. There is joy in chasing a dream.

Dreams don't have to be major, but they sometimes are. Frank Wells, former president of Walt Disney Company, wanted a challenge after he passed age 50. He hadn't been a mountain climber, but he set out to climb the seven highest peaks in the world.

Forrest Russell, Jr., of Albany, Georgia, was visiting his brother one day in Victoria, Canada. Out taking a walk, he picked up two popsicle sticks and sat down to carve them with a pen knife. That began a whole new hobby and career for the retired Nationwide Insurance employee.

Five years later, he now is a serious wood carver, attending schools and meetings across the country and creating detailed works of art out of blocks of bass wood.

11. Raise a little hell. One of the privileges of growing old is that acting a little crazy is looked upon as being eccentric. This is a joy reserved for someone with enough age to get away with it.

The people who take advantage of this seem to be the ones who make the most of their final years. Winston Churchill was classic in his candor, as were Eleanor Roosevelt and Harry Truman. And in more recent years, so was George Burns. What might be outrageous coming from a younger person can be charming when it comes from an aging one.

When someone is old enough, he can say about anything.

There's a story about Henry Ford when he was well into his 70s and many younger executives were trying to wrestle control from him at Ford Motor Company. Ford was a "late great" of sorts in that he didn't start his car company until he was into his 40s. Ford's competency had been challenged in court. When the opposing attorney asked him some questions about his knowledge of the business, Ford's answer was, "Give me two minutes, and I can have ten people in here who can answer any one of those questions."

12. Smile. Staying young is a matter of attitude. Keep a bright and shining one. There's an image of the old cranky man who lives on forever. It is hard to believe that someone like that would achieve greatness late in life.

So many people who laugh and make people laugh live on and on. Ageless comedians such as Milton Berle, Bob Hope, George Burns, and Red Skelton lived or are living long lives.

When our family was about to move to New York, Susan and an 80-year-old friend, Elizabeth Thompson, discussed the move. Susan told Miss Elizabeth that she was worried about being happy in New York. Miss Elizabeth asked, "Were you happy in Atlanta?" When Susan answered yes, Miss Elizabeth responded, "Then you'll be happy in New York." Even if they'd rather live somewhere else, happy people tend to stay happy wherever they are.

13. Hang around young people. The young possess energy and enthusiasm. The older person can bring wisdom and experience, making a mighty combination.

14. Do one thing really well. This sounds so simple, but older achievers do exactly what younger ones do. They focus on one thing and try to do it better than anyone else.

Geneva McDaniel was a 105-year-old aerobics teacher.

Leila Denmark was in her late 90s and still practicing medicine.

Elliott Galloway is still running marathons in his late 70s, a notable avocation that overshadowed his fame from starting a successful private school.

Hamilton Lokey, after a successful law practice, reached new heights as a skydiver in his 80s.

Sarah Garrett Adams became a yoga expert at 90 after having been confined to a wheelchair a half dozen years earlier.

Baseball fan. Aerobics teacher. Doctor. Marathon runner. Skydiver. Yoga practitioner. Each does one thing that is exceptional and does it very well.

– – – – –

Those are my rules for success after 50. I haven't had time to try them all myself. But that's my plan.

> *"I promise to keep on living as though I expect to live forever. Nobody grows old by merely living a number of years. Years may wrinkle the skin, but to give up wrinkles the soul."*
>
> — Douglas MacArthur

LOOK AT THE PERSON NEXT TO YOU

You can find people who keep their focus on the future all around you. I can just glance across the hall into the office next to mine.

I look like I'm over 50. In my mind's eye, I'm still that dashing young man with a full head of hair and keen eyesight. However, in photos I am somewhat pudgy, wear glasses, and don't have much hair. I match my idea of an aging male. And I'm reminded of that daily.

First, my wife is regularly taken to be my daughter (as in, "We've missed seeing you and your three daughters lately." "I only have two daughters," I explain). One month younger than I am, Susan just looks girlish. It must be the hairdresser. Someday I'll get one, too. I just need to get some hair first.

Then, there is my business partner and friend, Paul Beckham, of the growing (and delightfully entertaining) marketing firm of Hope-Beckham, Inc.

Paul and I met when I was in my 20s. He controlled the budget for the nutty promotions I dreamed up for Turner's Atlanta Hawks and

Braves. After working together on extravaganzas like a leap into the world's largest salad to find keys to win an automobile, or a dive into a giant bowl of ice cream, or pre-game ostrich racing, Paul and I became lifelong friends.

My business partner, Paul Beckham, and me

It wasn't until lately, though, that Paul's age became an issue. We were traveling down I-85 from Charlotte to Atlanta and pulled off the road to stop for lunch. We ordered the same thing. Mine cost a dollar less. Without asking, the waitress had given me the senior citizens discount. She didn't give it to Paul, who is three years older. When I told the waitress he was older, she said, "No way."

In his mid-50s, Paul is an adventurer and always has a new and exciting plan going. Well, some are just new, others are exciting — like going to Costa Rica to check out real estate or figuring out how to own a company plane for less than it costs to fly commercial.

Before we became partners, he went through an emotional grind that thousands of workers face when turning 50. Paul was formerly an executive at Turner Broadcasting System, in fact, one of Ted Turner's top lieutenants for twenty-three years. He started when Turner Broadcasting was very small, and his position grew as the company grew. His opinion always counted, and he played significant roles in Turner's purchases of the Atlanta Braves and Atlanta Hawks as well as in the startups of the "Super Station" (Channel 17) and CNN.

People at Turner Broadcasting would say that the only three numbers Ted Turner understood on a financial statement were how much money came in, how much went out, and how much was left. Paul knew the rest.

Then, suddenly, after twenty-three years on the job, Paul was no longer needed.

"It's a cost-age ratio," he states philosophically. "That's what downsizing is. You replace an older expensive employee with someone who is young and less expensive. You may lose a little on performance, but you save a lot of money.

"It's a very emotional thing to be told you're no longer needed," he adds. "You may tell them to make you an offer, and you will consider leaving if it is good enough, but you don't want them to agree with you and actually make that offer."

He is well situated financially, having been key to the success of the Turner empire. So he could have sat back and done nothing the rest of his life.

But that's not Paul. He charged ahead into life with more vigor than ever.

He started karate lessons and became a black belt three years later. He bought two old wooden boats and is refinishing them. He bought a Harley-Davidson motorcycle and sometimes rides it to work. He became certified as a scuba diver.

"You ask yourself, 'Can you still do it?'" he says about his venture into karate. "Can you take on a 22-year-old and win? The answer is 'yes.'"

He even started remodeling his house. "Remodeling a house at age 50 is a statement in itself that you are looking to the future, not dwelling on the past," he notes.

"Getting old is a downward spiral," he continues. "If you stop doing things, it gets harder to start back doing them again. I have some 40-year-old friends who are old, but I don't want to be old. I don't feel any different than I did twenty years ago."

Having friends who are old in age but young in spirit is important to Paul. One friend got into the business of raising llamas at age 65. Another quit work at age 55 to travel the world. Another got married in his 70s. "Before getting married," Paul remembers, "we went to the Masters golf tournament. He brought his girlfriend along. It started raining, and they went back to the car. When I got to the car, the windows were all steamed up. I was afraid to check and see what was going on. He was like a kid."

Paul has also jumped into his new business with enthusiasm. We formed Hope-Beckham, Inc., three years ago. He balances his work with other business ventures, as well as his hobbies.

"Changing to a new job brings a freshness both to you and the job," he says. "Someone said you should change jobs every five years. That's probably true. I'm just as enthusiastic now as I've ever been but I'm a hell of a lot better because I've seen a lot more. The best thing a person can bring to a job is good decisions. How do you learn to make good decisions? By having made bad decisions in the past.

"The trick is to be flexible and apply your experience to new things," he continues. "You have to be able to move away from having two secretaries to doing work by yourself on your own computer."

Another secret to Paul's agelessness may be the ability to know when to take life seriously and when not to. The 1937 U.S. Open Golf Tournament had been played in Pelham, New York, and when I lived there, Paul and I would head out on the greens every time he came to town. The results were unprecedented in my golfing career.

When I hit a golf ball into the woods, I would search for it in frustration until I'd finally give up and painfully drop a new ball in its spot. When Paul hit a ball astray, he'd just casually drop a new one and pretend the former had never existed. He wasted no time getting anxious over something as trivial as a golf ball. After I shot a nine on a par four hole, he asked me how I thought I might have done if I had not hit the drive off to the right and in the woods. I told him a six would have been achievable. He pulled out the scorecard and gave me a six. After all, Paul noted, it was only a game to be played for fun. When Susan studied the card and said, "You did better than you usually do," Paul just winked and never said a word.

Or, it may be that Paul's long marriage keeps him young.

"I read somewhere that the most successful people in America are still married to their first wives," he notes. "I don't know if it's true, but it should be. Marriage says a lot about a person's staying power, the ability to stick with something until it's done. In marriage, your partner can drive you crazy on Tuesday and then you can love her on Thursday. If you stick with marriage, it works. If you stick with life, it works. There is a similarity.

"You need someone to hang onto in life, someone who is there with you to share the experiences. That's part of the journey, part of being alive."

Paul's an inspiration to me. Do you have a "next-door" role model to keep you going strong?

> *"Perhaps one has to be very old before one learns how to be amused rather than shocked."*
>
> — Pearl S. Buck

A SEARCH FOR SOMETHING

All of us who consider ourselves normal and stable watch curiously as our friends go through the "midlife crisis." Men jump ship from their wives of decades to run off with young chicks. Someone will drop out of life and sail around the world.

When I worked at Burson-Marsteller, I had a friend named Bill Noonan. Bill was 56 years old and had been one of the real stars of the company. As it did with others over 50, the company appeared to be phasing him out of the mainstream of operations. His title remained president of the international division, but he was no longer considered one of the real players.

Bill was a tall, slim, soft-spoken man with silky gray hair and glasses. He had adult children and lived by himself in Manhattan. He seemed lonely. His wife had died a couple of years earlier of cancer.

The 13th floor at Burson-Marsteller was where the top executives worked. The average age on the floor was about 60. All the top executives were male, and all secretaries were female. Most of the secretaries were also older women, except for one named Alice. Alice was a 26-year-old bombshell. She was about six feet tall and didn't quite fit the sedate demeanor of the entire floor.

One day I was traveling and checked in with our receptionist, Sally, for my messages.

When I asked if anything was going on at the office, Sally told me the big news of the day. Alice, the 26-year-old bombshell of the office, was marrying 56-year-old Bill Noonan. I was stunned.

Bill and Alice Noonan and kids

Middle-age crazy and trophy wives were things I had seen, but the disease had never struck this close to home. The engagement kept the gossip channels full for weeks. Bill was more than old enough to be her father.

On their wedding night, a horse-drawn carriage took them from the church to their reception, traveling through one of the riskier areas of Harlem to get there. "As the carriage passed through Harlem, people were coming out of their stores to cheer us and wish us luck," Bill remembers. "However, I remember one man yelling up to me, 'You married to her, man? She gonna kill you, man.'"

The marriage has been a great one. "I couldn't be happier," Bill told me after celebrating his ninth wedding anniversary with Alice.

Bill always seems to have more vigor and zest than other men his age.

"Young women can do that to you," he laughs.

"It's been a terrific experience," he says. "The kids have been a real treat. When my first four were growing up, I was working and traveling. I never seemed to have the time to spend with them. Somehow, I am enjoying these two more and spending the time with them that I wish I had spent with the others. They've given me a new enthusiasm for life."

He also says he's had the money and time to enjoy Alice in a way he'd never been able to enjoy his first marriage.

"I make good money now, and I'm not struggling to build a career like I was in my first marriage," he said. "We took a trip on the Orient Express, and we've been on a cruise of the Greek Isles. Our life together has been a real joy. No one says anything about our age difference. We never talk about it ourselves. In fact, it sounds trite, but we've never had an argument."

In past times, I would have argued against such a match. Bill Noonan is approaching his 65th birthday, and he recently found out he has leukemia. The likelihood of him seeing his two small children grow to adulthood is probably fairly slim. But the likelihood of him thoroughly enjoying the remainder of his life seems to be brighter than ever.

Bill and Alice Noonan made me rethink the whole idea of May/December relationships.

> *"We must not measure greatness from the mansion down,
> but from the manger up."*
>
> — Jesse Jackson

TOUCHED BY GRACE

A teenager haunted by bad experiences does not understand why her world is cruel and out of control. A woman of 50 understands many cruelties all too well. And she can do something about them.

Several years ago we had dinner with some friends. The husband was president of one of America's leading companies. His spouse had been the model corporate wife for more than twenty years. During dinner, she said something unusual enough for me to remember years later. We were discussing how each of us had met our spouses.

She said she was in a bar one night and saw her future husband in a windbreaker with a "crimson H." The H was for Harvard, and she knew a Harvard man could be her meal ticket for life. "I moved right in and introduced myself."

It was a casual dinner comment but seemed out of character.

"I married him because I thought he could take care of me, that I'd have a good life," she said recently, "the life I had missed out on up to that point."

Not long ago, an announcement arrived in the mail. My wife and I were invited to the graduation of the lady from seminary and her ordination into the ministry. Now past age 50, she had become a certified member of the clergy.

Why would the wife of a successful business leader become an ordained minister? For that matter, her ministry was with abused women in one of America's most dangerous downtown areas. Each day she was putting her life in danger, going out on inner-city streets where notorious street gangs roamed. She worked with abused women and their children in the midst of those who were abusing them, people who often seemed to put very little value on any life. That sounded like work for younger people.

"My goals have changed every five years or so," she says. "When I first got married, I wanted to be well known. I wanted people to see me and say 'wow' and think how accomplished I was. I wanted power and position.

"Like so many other women, I was always seeking a nicer house, a nicer car, more notoriety."

I didn't know her when she was in her 20s, but she must have been a real beauty. Her dark complexion, strong chin, and chiseled features give her a look of elegance and strength. Past 50, she is a very distinguished-looking and lovely woman. Her posture is erect and confident. Everything about her demeanor suggests strength.

"I wanted to be the good corporate wife," she says. "I looked great on the outside, but I'd go to an event with my husband and come home thinking I had blown it. Some way, I thought, I had done something wrong or said something that I shouldn't have said. I wasn't happy with who I was or what I was trying to be."

When I first called to suggest an interview for this book, she declined. The story she would have to tell was too private. And she said, she didn't want to hurt her mother. She quickly agreed to be included as long as her name was withheld. It was not important to her to be known, but it was important to her that people who grew up in similar circumstances hear what she had to say. So, here's the sensitive part of her story.

This perfect picture of a corporate wife had been an illegitimate child, verbally and physically abused by her mother and sexually abused by her stepfather. She had a miserable childhood.

She attended thirteen different grammar schools. Because of scar tissue from an operation, she was deaf from age 3 to 6. She could talk, and she interpreted the words of others by reading their lips. Because of these abilities, her mother and other adults all too often saw her as misbehaving, not just unable to hear. The result was pain at the hands of the ones she needed love from the most.

"Your mother should not be the one to turn against you," she reflects. "Wounds suffered at the hand of your mother are the worst wounds of all. You feel cheated that you don't have a role model to look up to. You worry when you have your own kids."

Her husband was the first person to display unconditional love for her. He was a real hero for her. But still, her challenges with what she felt she should be and what she finally became were long and agonizing. As a new member of an upper-middle-class, successful family, she had a choice of simply relaxing in her good life or giving back.

She joined civic leadership programs in different cities as her husband was promoted and moved. Yet, she wasn't satisfied with her life. She wasn't even completely in touch with what was causing her unhappiness.

"Children who are abused grow up thinking they are unattractive, that something must be wrong with them or they wouldn't be treated so badly," she observed. "When I was young, I would try to make myself look unattractive, thinking that if I were ugly, my stepfather as well as others would leave me alone. My mother controlled the way I dressed, so I would compensate with bad posture and misbehavior, anything I could do to seem ugly or undesirable. I didn't want to be hurt."

She suppressed the memories of her childhood, and they didn't return to her until her own daughter reached the age she had been when first abused. She started having dreams of what had happened. Finally, the "black box" of dreadful memories emerged vividly and changed the remainder of her life.

As successful and confident as she appeared on the surface, the self-doubt continued to fester. She had a nervous breakdown when her children were young. "I wasn't equipped to be a mom. I had no role model growing up. My mother didn't make her mistakes on purpose. Sometimes I would say and do things to my own children, leave the room, and break down and cry, asking for forgiveness for what I had just said or done."

In her difficult emotional battles, the man she selected as her husband purely for material reasons became her spiritual ally. A rough-and-tumble character in business, her husband was gentle and deeply religious underneath. He was raised in a devout Catholic family.

"At that time in our lives, we would be invited to Bible studies. He would want to go, but I would refuse. I thought the Bible was a dead book. I was very cynical about it all.

"One day, a friend who was heavily involved in my political activities invited me to a Bible study at her house. I went because of who she was. She was bright and successful. I was mystified that a well-educated group of women in a classy house were gathering to study the Bible."

Always outspoken, she told her friends what she thought of the meeting. "This stuff may be okay for Bible bangers, but I can't buy into it," she said.

"But I went home feeling a real yearning," she remembers. "These women were smart, and they had found something. Why did such well-educated women believe so much in what was in this old book?

"Several weeks later I got on my knees and said, 'God, I don't know who you are but I know that I can no longer do it all myself. I surrender. I need you in my life.' At that point, I became a Christian."

When the couple moved to their current city, their children were grown. She no longer had the challenge of being the mother of the household. She was ready to make her big move. Approaching 50, she started volunteering as a counselor for abused women.

The challenges were frustrating. The government moved one 32-year-old woman and her child into a $600-a-month apartment with a pool.

They were on welfare, which would soon run out. She knew there was no way they could pay for the apartment. Situations like that seemed hopeless.

"One night I dropped off a teenage girl at her home at midnight," she said. "No one was at home, she didn't have a key. She couldn't get in her own house. I thought that even in my childhood, I could get in my house. I had a place to go."

She quickly found that she needed the right credentials to achieve success with her new challenges. Volunteers were not appreciated. They were often viewed as threats to paid workers, and when the time came to address a real crisis, a volunteer typically couldn't even get in the door of government offices, hospitals, halfway houses, and jails.

"There is respect for the clergy in the inner city," she said. "I can go anywhere and be safe, and I can get into the places I need to go, whether it's jail or the halfway homes where women are sent to be protected. They are very cautious about allowing strangers in, but the clergy has the sanction. The clergy has the credentials necessary to get where they need to go to do the things that need to be done."

Her venture into religious ordination was also an adventure into learning.

"Going to seminary was a way to learn the Scripture and interpret it for myself, and find out what the Greek and Hebrews really meant when they wrote it. I didn't want to depend on what others told me about the Bible. I wanted to be able to read it in its original version and make up my own mind."

While she studied for her seminary degree, her husband edited her papers. She's dyslexic, and reading was a real struggle. "I would read things over and over before I'd comprehend what was on the paper in front of me. I was often exhausted and out of energy. Yet, I was encouraged by my professors, my husband, and my many friends."

Now, ordained, she is a pastor of women, not men. She's on the streets fighting their unique battles. She even thanks the Lord for her childhood, saying, "Who else can better understand the problems of battered young women than me?"

"Many older people have given up on their own values and morals and conceded to the younger generations," she concludes. "There are so many great things that older people can do. It's hard, but they need to do them.

"I don't know how long I can keep doing what I'm doing. We could be called to move again to another city. But every day I spend is a chance to make a difference. What I'm doing is a growing process. It's lifelong. When people ask me what I want to achieve, I point them to the Scripture. Someday I hope to stand before Jesus and hear him say, 'Well done, good and faithful servant.'"

How has she dealt with her mother, who is living in a Florida senior citizens facility? She and her husband provide financial assistance.

"When I graduated, I gave her a copy of my diploma. For all she did, she's still proud of me."

"How old would you be if you didn't know how old you was?"

— Satchel Paige

A PASSION FOR A NEW GAME

Like many men, I have battled with the relationship of women to my world. One of the many bizarre promotions I held for the Atlanta Braves (the promotions for which I was inducted into the Baseball Hall of Shame) was the world's largest wet T-shirt contest.

Ted Turner once began a speech with the words, "I was happy to be invited here by Bob Hope. Bob and I both are proof that you do things in your 20s that you don't do in your 40s." So true.

The years, and my beautiful wife and daughters, have taught me many lessons.

I have since become an avid booster for women's sports opportunities. Hope-Beckham helped the women's American Basketball League get started. We have been working with the National Soccer Alliance, a planned pro league for women. I am a supporter of the Women's Sports Foundation and go to its annual banquet each year in New York. Paul and I attend the Women In Sports and Entertainment (WISE) luncheon and seem to be accepted as full-fledged members, even if we inherently don't qualify for membership.

And I was inducted into the U.S. Women's Sports Hall of Fame for starting the Silver Bullets baseball team in 1993.

I want to tell the story of the Silver Bullets, but not my story. I want to tell about Phil Niekro, baseball hall-of-famer and the greatest knuckleball pitcher of all time.

Phil Niekro

I've known Phil Niekro since I was 18 years old. That means thirty-three years. He pitched in the big leagues until he was 48 years old. He was a Braves player for twenty of his twenty-four major league years. He set a major league record for winning games after age 40 while on his way to a total of 318 victories — the 14th best record in history. At age 58, he still swore he could pitch and win for a big league team.

After being released by the Braves at age 44, he went on to win thirty-two more games in two seasons with the New York Yankees. His final win for the Yankees was the 300th of his career. Yankees owner George Steinbrener had told him he felt his career was over, that the only pitch he could throw any more was his fabled knuckleball, which seldom traveled over 60 miles an hour from the pitcher's mound to home plate, compared to the 90-mile-an-hour speed of younger pitchers. Phil showed Steinbrener by winning his 300th game without throwing a single knuckleball until the final pitch, which he threw for a strikeout to finish the game. "I was making up pitches as the game went along," he said.

While Phil pitched his 300th victory, his dad (a coal miner who had taught the knuckleball to Phil and his brother) lay in a coma in an Ohio hospital. Phil had been with him until the day of the game. His father wasn't expected to wake up from the coma and doctors said he might die at any moment. Phil Sr.'s wife, Ivy, listened to the game over a telephone line and gave her silent husband a report pitch by pitch. When his son struck out the final batter, the elder Niekro opened his eyes and said, "He did it." It was the first time he had been awake in weeks. The next time Phil and his brother Joe saw their dad, he was sitting in a rocking chair, and he lived to see both sons complete their big league careers.

Phil has always amazed me with his conviction to do what is right. It is popular today to say kids no longer have any sports role models. Whether or not that's true, there sure aren't many around like Phil. While he was playing baseball, he would always volunteer to help charities, and unlike other players, he'd jump right in and help with the work.

One day in 1975, Phil cornered me in the Braves clubhouse before a game. He told me he was state chairman of the Big Brothers Association. He explained that Big Brothers provided male father figures to young boys who didn't have dads. He wanted me to be a Big Brother. When he explained that I had to take a kid someplace every week, I thought, "No way." But Phil persisted, and I signed up.

For the next ten years, I was Big Brother to Phillip Lewis, a boy who had lost his dad in an auto accident. Phillip became part of our family.

Niekro got me into that. In 1993, Phil returned the favor.

In the summer of 1984, I watched a lot of softball with my two daughters. We would see both men and women play, and some of the women seemed very capable of playing baseball. If they played softball so well, I wondered why they didn't play the "real thing."

The next spring, we held tryouts for a team to be called the Sun Sox, which we wanted to put into a class A men's minor league. We had talked to the Florida State League, which had an opening in Daytona Beach. Of course, we had no money.

At the tryouts, Georgia Tech baseball coach Jim Morris analyzed the group of forty and said that six might qualify as minor league prospects. But one had the physical quickness and strength of a male big league prospect. Furman Bisher, a local newspaper columnist, called her "The Natural." She looked like a baseball player.

Hank Aaron came to see the tryouts that day. "The Natural" was warming up.

"That's a player," he said. Then, he remarked that she had a make-up compact, in her back pocket.

"That's not make-up," someone said. "It's a baseball."

"It's too small to be a baseball," Hank noted.

I finally walked out to check it out. She had a tin of snuff in her rear pocket.

She was a ballplayer in every sense of the term.

There seemed to be evidence that women could play baseball if they wanted to play.

I presented the idea of a women's baseball team to a lot of people over the years. Most of the time I got laughed out of meetings when I'd bring it up. Finally, someone alerted me that Coors Brewing Company was concerned about its sexist image. It used bikini-clad women in its advertising, for instance. As a way to combat that image, the president of the company, Leo Kiely, gave us $50,000 and two months to figure out how to put together a viable team.

After getting major league baseball and the Women's Sports Foundation to support the idea, we had to find the right manager to lead the team, as well as the right coaches. There were no qualified women's coaches, of course.

We needed credibility. Ideally, the manager would be someone who had made a name for himself in major league baseball.

I made my list of people who could do the job. Phil Niekro was the only one on that list. He was the only one I knew.

Phil had invested well and made plenty from his major league pension. At 53, he lived on Lake Lanier in Flowery Branch, Georgia, about forty miles from Atlanta. He kept busy with his charity work and also fished and played a lot of golf. He didn't need the job, especially not for the salary we could pay.

I thought there might be just one way to convince him. Phil has immense respect for people as well as for the game of baseball. The idea could appeal to him that women might be able to play baseball, and the only thing keeping them from it has been no one stepping forward to give them a chance.

I called him to ask him whether he would consider managing a women's baseball team. His answer was short and brief. "Nope, I don't think so."

He did tell me that his sister Phyllis was his catcher in the backyard when he was growing up and that she was better than most of the boys in town. Because of Phyllis he had always wondered how good women could be as baseball players.

When I called him a couple of months later to tell him we were moving ahead with the team, he had made up his mind. He wanted to give girls and women a chance to play baseball. He just wanted assurance that it would be pure baseball. He said, "I have too much respect for the game to have it any other way."

Also, he noted, "There are only so many fish you can catch and golf balls you can hit when you retire. I want a challenge."

Since there were no women's teams to play, the only option was to play against men, who had been playing baseball all their lives. It would be a tough season. The Silver Bullets lost their first game to the Northern League All-Stars 19-0 and didn't score a run in their first five games.

They lost thirty-eight games and won only six that first season. Through it all, Phil gave them encouragement.

He managed the team as if it were a big league contender, showing the women respect as both people and ballplayers. Once, in San Antonio, a public address announcer thought it would be clever to call the women lesbians. Phil had him removed from the ballpark.

When Phil talked about his three sons, he would also tell people he now had twenty-four daughters.

On the final day of that first season, the Silver Bullets played at Atlanta Fulton-County Stadium, where Phil pitched most of his career.

Phil told the players how proud he was of them for battling together to make history. They had shown more pride and respect for the game of baseball than any group he had ever seen.

"I get interviewed by sportswriters in every city when we play a game," he continued. "Some of them look at me like the drunk old ballplayer that Tom Hanks played in *A League of Their Own*. I tell them I have plenty of other things I could be doing, but this is where I want to be. If they want to know why I'm here, I tell them the answer comes every time one of you makes a great play or gets a hit. If someone weren't willing to step forward and give you that opportunity, it could never happen."

There is crying in baseball. It took place that day.

When Phil Niekro was inducted into the Baseball Hall of Fame in 1997, he had the Silver Bullets team on the front row. He had them there, he said, "because I want to show the world that baseball is not a game for just men and boys. It's a game for everyone."

The greatest knuckleball pitcher of all time, Phil is in the Baseball Hall of Fame for what he did before age 50. However, he might just as well have been inducted for what he's done after age 50 because that's when he opened the doors of baseball to half the world. He has put his heart on the line to give women a chance to play the game he loves.

And, by the way, Phil's team finished last season, it's fourth, with a winning record. The women really *can* play baseball.

> *"The man who views the world at 50 the same as he did at 20 has wasted thirty years of his life."*
>
> — Muhammad Ali

THE LATEST ON "THE GREATEST"

The moment Muhammad Ali lit the Olympic caldron at the 1996 Summer Olympics was one of the most memorable in sports history. At the opening ceremonies, I sat about twenty yards away from the ramp up which Ali, stricken with Parkinson's disease, slowly walked to light the flame. He seemed to stand forever trembling, trying to light the fuse that would carry the flame to the giant torch. The slow and precarious journey of the flame made Ali's trembling all that more notable.

I'd had lunch with Ali twenty years before when Ted Turner stuck his head into my office and asked me to go with him to the Stadium Club at Atlanta-Fulton County Stadium. It was the first time either Ted or I had met Ali.

Ali, already retired as a boxer, showed the same manic energy that made him a world-reknowned figure during his career. Ted told the former world champ about an idea he had for his "Super Station," Channel 17. "Let me go in the ring against you on TV," he said. "You know, it will be sort of like one of those contests where the man wrestles a bear. We'll do it just for fun. Nobody will get hurt."

Ali sat back and listened to Ted's excited spiel. He responded, "Mr.

Turner, you're crazier than you look."

After the 1996 Olympics, I had lunch with Ali again to plan for the first Ali Cup International Boxing Challenge in his hometown of Louisville, Kentucky. It was a different Ali. Because of his Parkinson's disease, he often dozed while we ate. He was smartly dressed in a gray shirt and slacks, but food had spilled down the front. His wife, Lonnie, related what Muhammad might say about various topics, if he could speak loud enough for us to hear.

Muhammad Ali at the Ali Cup

His face and body were puffy, either from medication or his malady. I was told his appearance was misleading. Despite looking distant and unaware, he was taking it all in and fully understood.

Lonnie said Ali had come up with the idea for the Ali Cup, an amateur boxing tournament. At 55 years old, he wanted to give back to the sport that allowed him to gain fame and wealth. Boxing had brought him from a poor Louisville neighborhood to become one of the most famous humans on Earth.

More than forty years earlier, a youngster named Casius Clay was picked up by a policeman, Joe Martin, and taken to a gym to learn to box. Casius rose through the ranks of amateur boxing to win a gold medal at the Olympics in Rome in 1960. He was heavyweight champion of the world three different times.

Our company had been hired to promote the Ali Cup as well as a giant entertainment tribute that would take place on the night following the finals.

The plans were bold. The Ali Cup would be the first international boxing tournament ever held in the United States other than the Olympics. The best ninety-six boxers from more than thirty countries would come to Louisville to compete for a week. It would feature the boxers who had won medals at the 1996 Olympics in Atlanta.

The event also included a Muhammad Ali Tribute to Amateur Boxing. The combination of celebration and concert took place in 22,000-seat Freedom Hall. It was a big league celebration of a major, even if bruised, sport.

The Muhammad Ali Tribute to Amateur Boxing was a marvelous event in many ways. Natalie Cole, James Earl Jones, and Jeff Foxworthy performed. Evander Holyfield boxed against University of Kentucky basketball coach Tubby Smith in a fantasy bout. Former world heavyweight champ Jimmy Ellis boxed against University of Louisville coach Denny Crum. Foxworthy fought Olympic gold-medal winner David Reid. When Ali went into the ring against the 13-year-old state champion of South Carolina, the crowd roared with the chant of "Ali, Ali, Ali, Ali." Ali came out of his lethargy, and his personality lit up for a few moments as he did his old Ali shuffle and sparred with the youngster. He finally picked the boy up and gently placed him on the mat, raising his arms in victory. The crowd loved it.

It was a wonderful experience for everyone.

At each boxing competition, Ali would sit in a chair at ringside signing autographs as long as people would ask for them. He sat there for hours.

A meeting was set for him to meet a woman whose son had recently been killed on the streets of Louisville. When Ali heard that the press had been invited, he asked for privacy. Not being able to talk, he simply held the hand of the woman to express his sympathy. He showed her magic tricks. In a day when people fight for publicity, he was avoiding it for all the right reasons.

During the day of the tribute the boxers from around the world were introduced in a pregame ceremony before a sellout crowd of 45,000 at the University of Louisville football game against no. 1 Penn State. Starting faintly, the chant of the crowd grew. Soon, everyone was on their feet, yelling "Ahaaa-leeee, Ahaaa-leee, Ahaaa-leee, Ahaaaa-leee." It was a magic moment. The man once known for words could no longer say a thing. Body trembling, he raised one arm in a gesture of recognition.

He was still the greatest.

"It's better to be a lion for a day than a sheep all your life."
— Sister Elizabeth Kenny

DIVING OFF THE DEEP END

EDGARD BARRETO

"Where did we lose the 'piss and vinegar'? When did we lose it?" 60-year-old Edgard Barreto asked.

He was trying to explain why he was playing college football for Ashland (Ohio) University with players who were forty years his junior.

When I read about the old man who had asked for a tryout with a college football team, I thought him completely nuts, one of those people who were doing things that made no sense at all. It seemed an aberration, something that probably had no more meaning than a publicity stunt or losing a bet. After talking to him, I changed my mind. What he was doing made more sense than what most other 60-year-olds might be doing.

Previously, Ed had been a physics, chemistry, and biology teacher at Edison Junior College in Fort Myers, Florida, where he was also the soccer coach. He's always been a "contrarian." He credits his different way of thinking to his native country, Brazil.

"Our family doesn't define success the way people from America define success," he says. "In the United States, most people define success based on their business achievements. You start life delivering newspapers. Then you buy a bike so you can deliver more newspapers. You then buy a car so you can deliver even more newspapers. It never stops. Pretty soon you have a Mercedes to deliver papers, and you can't understand why you're not happy. People here work too hard and don't enjoy their lives."

Ed and his family work hard but in different ways and for different reasons.

One year, Ed ran 101 races — two every weekend.

Ed's run 238 marathons in his lifetime.

In 1983, he, his wife, Sandra, and their three teenage daughters ran from Ocean City, Maryland, to San Diego, California.

His latest challenge is playing college football while studying for his master's degree in sports sciences at Ashland University, a Division II NCAA school. He is a substitute defensive back for the Ashland Eagles. He played two seasons as a special teams player when he was an undergraduate at the school in the 1950s.

This new challenge started when he decided to take up gardening.

Last year Ed purchased a plot of land in his hometown of Naples, Florida. He and Sandra lived in a condominium but Ed wanted enough land to plant a garden.

"I told my family I was ready to do some gardening and become a peaceful old man," he says.

"My wife got mad," he continues. "She said I was giving up on life. She told me I was going to grow old, get sick, get high blood pressure, and become an old grouch. We were joking when we first talked about me going out for the football team, but it grew to being a challenge."

He was recovering from a pulled hamstring muscle when I talked to him but planned to be back at full speed for the next game, which would be homecoming. He was also going to be the grand marshal of the homecoming parade.

"I want to keep my spunk," he laughs. "There is nothing easy about what I'm doing. These guys are strong, fast, and very hard to keep up with. They're also nice and having a lot of fun."

"Why do we lose our 'piss and vinegar'?" he asks again. "It has nothing to do with growing old. It is because of all the folks who beat us down. It's because we focus on material things and never have enough of them."

As teachers, both Ed and Sandra "tried to build self-confidence, discipline, and morals with the kids. We tried to do it by doing things a little different," Ed says. Football is another outlet for that.

"I love working with the kids, and I think I am doing more for them by example than I ever could do trying to teach them. They all seem to enjoy having me on the team."

What's next after football for Edgard and family?

"We've talked about running the Great Wall of China."

FARRAH FAWCETT

I first met Jane Fonda when she was dating Ted Turner in 1990. Almost everyone who meets Jane comes away making the same comments. She is classy and polite. However, for a woman well into her 50s, she has a strange artificial look of youth. She's beautiful but seemingly not all real.

I assumed Farrah Fawcett must be the same way.

No one was more popular than Farrah Fawcett in the middle and late 1970s when the TV show "Charlie's Angels" was a hit. A pose of the bathing-suit-clad beauty graced the walls of college dorms and fraternities throughout the country.

Her hairstyle, with lots of long strands of hair somewhat out of control, was nearly as distinctive as the Beatles' haircuts were a decade earlier. Her hair set a standard that was mimicked by young women who wanted to be Farrah Fawcett. When I was working for the Braves, we had a Farrah Fawcett look-a-like contest on the field prior to a game. Hundreds of women showed up to compete.

Farrah Fawcett

Bette Davis once said "old age is no place for sissies." That idea is especially true for people who have relied on good looks for a living.

When I heard that Farrah Fawcett at age 50 was using her nude body as a brush to make paintings, my reaction was similar to when I watched Mike Tyson bite off Evander Holyfield's ear in the heavyweight championship bout. I couldn't figure out what to think.

On top of that, it was announced that Farrah Fawcett would appear in *Playboy* nude, demonstrating her best paint-with-naked-body skill. And a home video of the painting process would be on the shelves of the local video stores.

Wow. I guess it doesn't hurt anyone, but it was a little hard to stomach. The issues of women's rights seemed complex enough without a 50-year-old female stepping in to showcase herself as an aging sex object.

Farrah Fawcett appeared on the "Late Show with David Letterman" one night trying to explain her art. I watched it. She fumbled around and really made no sense. I was not enlightened.

So, I bought the issue of *Playboy*. I don't want to sound prudish or out of touch, but it was the first copy of the magazine I had purchased since college.

"Farrah, All of Me" was the title of the article.

She was described as the "foxiest action painter in art history."

The article follows the history of the unique form of art, noting that French artist Yves Klein (1928–1962) used naked women as his brushes. He would "drag them across canvases to the accompaniment of his own musical composition."

Farrah in the artistic process

Farrah, by the way, is an artist by trade, in addition to being an actress. She studied art and sculpture at the University of Texas. She said she had always wanted to paint with her body.

"Historically, Americans have been known to have a problem with both art and nudity," she was quoted in the article. "In Europe, people seem to be much more open toward art and the body. I studied Renaissance art and have always admired the relationship between art and the body."

In discussing why she is doing it at age 50, she said, "I've grown and I've developed the courage and conviction to get this done. I'm basically a shy person."

If the idea was odd, the photos looked good. She was every bit as attractive as she was two decades ago. I appreciate someone the same age as I am looking that good.

In the magazine photos, she is covered in gold and looks like a bronze statue of a much younger woman.

"You don't feel quite so nude wearing paint," she said.

The author of the article wrote, "Somehow, judging from these pictures and the film of Farrah painting, one tends to believe her. She is genuinely into it. It's not acting. That rapt quality makes her presence exponentially more exotic than a woman consciously doing something overtly sexual."

As I said, I don't know what to think on this one. It is pioneering. It's not doing what an older woman is expected to do. It's not accepting aging gracefully or even at all.

Who am I to judge?

On another page in the magazine, Miss September 1963, Victoria Valentino, is featured in an article about the *Centerfold Sweethearts* newsletter she publishes. She keeps track of past Playmates for the Centerfold Alumni Association. Pictured in the short two-paragraph story is a photo of a nude young woman taken in 1963, with an inset photo of a dignified but aging executive with eyeglasses.

As they say, different strokes for different folks. Two old-timers took different roads, but one thing seems obvious; once a centerfold, always a centerfold.

VIOLA KRAHN

Viola Krahn literally dove off the deep end when she was 68 years old. That was in 1970 when she decided to take up competitive diving. Today, at 95, she is the U.S. Masters Outdoor Diving Champion.

"I'm having a wonderful time," she said after completing her four dives off the one-meter board to win the gold medal in Moultrie, Georgia. "Everyone here seems so happy and enthusiastic."

After beginning competitive diving at 19, she quit three years later in 1924 when she married Fred Cady, who coached American divers in the 1924, 1928, and 1932 Olympics. She started back again fifty-one years later when John Riley, a nationally known diver from San Diego, introduced her to the Masters diving program. She has appeared in every national Masters competition in the last twenty-seven years, winning most.

She's also competed in international competitions around the world. More active in the sport than ever, Viola is the most popular contestant wherever she competes.

"Viola is our most famous diver," said John Samuelson, a San Diego schoolteacher who attended the U.S. Masters Outdoor Diving Championships. "And she dives so beautifully."

Diving is not her only sport. For the past twelve years, she has spent two weeks a year riding horses at a dude ranch in Arizona.

Still driving, she frequently takes her car 150 miles from her home in Laguna Hills, California, to Santa Barbara, to visit her brother.

What's her antiaging secret?

"I still overdo candy and chocolates," she says. "But I sleep very well. My parents told me when I was younger to go to bed and go to sleep. I still do it.

"I don't think there's any secret. My father always said, do everything in moderation."

LILLIAN CARTER

Most Americans are familiar with President Jimmy Carter's work since he left office. He devotes considerable time to improving international relations through the Carter Center and to building Habitat for Humanity houses for people who might not otherwise be able to own a home. He has hammered away in city slums as well as in the most rural of areas, inspiring people throughout America to join in and volunteer. This altruistic work was started after President Carter left office at age 56 and has continued for the last seventeen years. If you wonder how he keeps going strong, look to his genes and lifelong example — his mom, Miss Lillian.

I met Lillian Carter when I brought the Braves to Plains on the week-

Ms. Lillian Carter and me in 1979

end before Jimmy Carter's presidential inauguration. The colorful Carter clan was in the media spotlight. Brother Billy, who ran a gas station in Plains, was becoming a national celebrity, even having his own brand of beer, Billy Beer. His sister, Ruth Carter Stapleton, was an outspoken evangelist (she was later featured in the movie *The People vs. Larry Flint* as the person who tried to change the ways of the infamous publisher of *Hustler* magazine.)

However, the most remarkable of all the Carters was the mother of the family, a nurse who had raised her children, lost her husband, and, in her 60s, joined the Peace Corps, serving as a volunteer in India.

We took the Braves to Plains to take on the Billy Carter All-Stars in softball. A crowd of about 5,000 surrounded the high school field as Braves players and front office people such as Hank Aaron and Phil

Niekro competed against Billy and his friends. Miss Lillian watched the entire game from a lawn chair near the first base line.

After that, she came to several Braves games during the next couple of seasons. Once, she was on hand to throw out the ceremonial first ball for an old-timers game, featuring former players from the Braves and Yankees.

I sat in the stadium club while she was having dinner following the event. During dinner, she worked on fixing up my secretary for a date with her state patrol bodyguard. When my somewhat reluctant secretary didn't have a business card to give to Ms. Carter, the president's mother took one of her checks as a source of her name and address. I got the impression that nothing slowed down Ms. Carter when she wanted something.

At one point, she asked me whether I would get her a refill of that nice drink, which she said, "looks like iced tea." I asked the bartender for another iced tea for Miss Lillian. "What do you mean?" he responded. "She's drinking straight bourbon." She was a feisty woman.

FILLING TIME WITH JOY

Bob Cohn, one of my best friends, is founder of Cohn & Wolfe, one of the largest and most successful public relations firms in the world. His company represents Coke, VISA, AT&T, the PGA, and about 100 other important organizations. Bob sold his business in 1984 and signed a contract that required him to keep working for three years. He is still there.

When I worked for Bob several years ago, we had a client, Worth Sports Company of Tullahoma, Tennessee, a small town halfway between Chattanooga and Nashville. Worth has been making softball, baseballs, and bats forever.

We drove up to Tullahoma quite often to meet with the president of Worth. At some point during the meeting, the chairman and owner of the company, Mr. Lannom, would stick his head into the meeting room to say hello. He never seemed to have much to do.

One day when Bob and I were driving to Worth, he said, "I've seen men like old man Lannom before. He has someone else running his business and comes to the office every day. He really doesn't have much to do, but he hangs around the office for a couple of hours and then leaves. He probably has lunch with the same people at the same place every day and drives a Jeep or pickup truck with a gun rack or golf clubs in the back so he can take off with his friends on a moment's notice. And I guarantee you he has some insane hobby. Something really far out, something he works hard on and is really proud of."

Bob and I were having our meeting at Worth that day when Mr. Lannom, for the first time, came in and invited us to go to lunch with him. We accepted.

As we left the building, Mr. Lannom asked whether we could drive because his Jeep wasn't big enough to hold all of us. He pointed to his Jeep, and I noted the gun rack on the back. Bob, I thought, was amazing. Mr. Lannom then directed us to the country club, where, he said, we would eat with the friends he met each day for lunch. Bob was a genius.

As we were driving back to his office, Mr. Lannom asked us whether we were in a hurry. He had something he wanted us to see.

He directed us to the Tullahoma airport and a giant hangar.

"I want to show you my hobby," he said with a smile.

Bob, I thought, was incredible.

Mr. Lannom was the world's top collector of a certain model biplane made in the 1930s. Planes of many different colors were spread throughout the hangar. Each had an elaborate display explaining its background.

I was impressed with the collection of planes, and I was more impressed with Bob's insight into human nature.

As Bob moved into his 50s, he got serious about a hobby, too.

In 1980, while working for Coke at the Winter Olympics in Lake Placid, New York, Bob discovered Olympic pin trading and collecting. He framed the pins he gathered along with photos of himself and his family at the Games.

His passion for pin collecting grew at the 1984 Olympics in Los Angeles.

Bob's interest expanded to other Olympic memorabilia, including torches and participation medals. He now has one of the half dozen most extensive collections of Olympic items in the world, including the world's top collection of torches, with one from every Olympic games.

Bob Cohn in Nagano

"I started trading and collecting the pins because it was a way to meet so many people at the Olympics, to start conversations," he says. "It opened doors to meet athletes and people from all over the world.

Cohn now has hundreds of thousands of Olympic pins. When the Olympics took place in Atlanta, he was active through his many clients who were sponsors of the Games. He was also a member of the Metropolitan Atlanta Olympic Governing Authority, appointed by the governor of Georgia. His hard work on the Olympics gave him inroads for his hobby. He was able to spend time in the athlete villages and the international press center to gather the hard-to-get country pins and media pins.

His collection is well known to Olympic memorabilia collectors throughout the world. He renovated the top floor of his home in an expensive Atlanta neighborhood to include an Olympic museum. Each item is displayed just as it might be in a public museum, with special cases and lighting.

"I'm 63 years old, and I haven't changed much over the past few years, other than I know that time is running out," he says. "I've had a couple of carcinomas and polyps removed. Sometimes it seems my body is attacking me inside and out. I know I'd better get done now what I want to do in my life.

"My business is creative, and every day is a completely new day," he continued. "I had one major career change, but that was when I was 37. That's when I left the newspaper business and started a public relations firm. I had no idea what I was doing. I just knew I wasn't going to make enough money as a newspaper reporter to support my family. It was a big jump."

His public relations firm now has twelve offices around the world.

"I wasn't brilliant but I was tenacious," he says. "The business has done far better than I ever dreamed. It really makes me feel good to go to places like London, Sydney, and Milan and know that my name is migrating around the world, that people are laboring in a business that has my name on the door. I want to see twenty Cohn & Wolfe offices before I'm through.

"I tell people that I'm older than Nolan Ryan, but I'm still pitching.

"I also want to enjoy the time I have left," he continues. "Sometimes I think I want to jump into something new in business, to run the flag up the pole one more time. But then I think I want to spend the time I have left with [my wife] June, doing the things we want to do.

"On Thursday morning, we decided to jump in the car and drive up to North Carolina to visit some old friends. I never would have left work like that before. I haven't even taken my full vacation time in the past.

"There are a lot of opportunities to refocus. We just became grandparents for the first time. June's mother was a grandparent at 39, and here I am for the first time at 63. They're going to have to wheel me out to his Little League games in a wheelchair, but I'm looking forward to it.

"I want to enjoy life, smell the roses."

"Nobody has ever measured, not even poets, how much the heart can hold."
— Zelda Fitzgerald

ONE MOMENT
THAT CHANGES
EVERYTHING

The ordinary life can become extraordinary with years of hard work and then one grand gesture near the end.

Ted Turner's pledge of a billion dollars to the United Nations, not to mention his business accomplishments at an age when many have retired, certainly qualifies him as "greater late" in his life than ever

Ted Turner

before.

But Ted's life has been a series of shocking and remarkable moves. In fact, a biography about his sailing adventures written when he was in his 30s is called *The Grand Gesture*. He's never been shy about getting attention. In one of my first meetings with him, he stood on his chair to rant about one topic, then jumped on top of a coffee table to make a point about another.

Not long ago, another grand gesture, again a monetary donation, came from a much more unlikely source. Showboats like Ted Turner shared the limelight for a while with a quiet washerwoman from Mississippi.

OSEOLA MCCARTY

At age 87, Oseola McCarty donated $150,000 to the University of Southern Mississippi. She didn't ask for anything in return, just that the money be used to send needy African-American children to college.

She had saved the money over the years from washing and ironing other people's clothes, depositing a few one-dollar bills at a time. In 1995, she asked her bank to give her life savings away.

"I want to help somebody's child go to college. I just want it to go to someone who will appreciate it and learn," she said.

Ms. McCarty dropped out of school at age 12 to care for a sick aunt.

"This is just extraordinary," said Aubrey Lucas, president of the school. "I don't know that I've ever been as touched by a gift to the university as I have been by this one."

Ms. McCarty has lived at the same small house on Miller Street in Hattiesburg, Mississippi, since 1947. She's never owned a car and only recently bought an air conditioner for her home. She has a small black-and-white TV (which she had never watched).

Her mother died in 1964, followed by her aunt three years later. Since then, she has lived by herself. People would bring their laundry to her but wouldn't stay to visit. Her only companions were a dog named Dog, a pig named Hog, and a cow named Hazel. She wore a simple smock with tennis shoes, the toes cut out. She was so painfully shy that she hardly ever said a word. Her arthritis forced her to retire at age 86.

Oseola McCarty

"I can't do everything," Ms. McCarty says, "but I can do something to help somebody. I wish I could do more."

The woman from America's Deep South had no way of knowing what her gift would mean. She was invited to visit President Clinton at the White House and receive the Presidential Citizens Medal. Because she had never flown, she traveled twenty-four hours on a train to get there.

Invitations to make appearances all over the country encouraged her to overcome her fear of flying. She was at Times Square on New Year's Eve to drop the ball to bring in the new year. Roberta Flack and Patti LaBelle sang "Amazing Grace" to her at a dinner in her honor.

The hotel maids in New York loved her because she was "one of their own."

Before her gift, she had been out of Mississippi only once.

"I'm braver now," she says. "I want to see. I want to know."

Most of her life she had no one to talk to, but she is quickly making up for that. She has been interviewed for the front page of the *New York Times* and featured as one of Barbara Walters's "10 Most Fascinating People." She's appeared on "Good Morning America" and even its counterpart in Argentina.

Harvard gave her an honorary doctorate. She carried the Olympic Torch. The Urban League and the National Institute of Social Sciences honored her. She won the Wallenberg Humanitarian Award.

A painting of her now hangs in the administration building of the University of Southern Mississippi.

Other people have donated $200,000 to her original gift.

Oseola McCarty remains a simple woman, buying only the things she needs.

Life in general is pretty simple in the terms of this humble laundress. "If you want to be proud of yourself, you have to do things you can be proud of," she says.

CAROLYN MCCARTHY

Some moments that change lives aren't planned or positive.

But, somehow, good evolves from the bad.

Carolyn McCarthy was a 50-year-old mother and nurse in Mineola, New York, a small village on Long Island. She was a backyard gardener with no political ambitions.

On December 7, 1993, her life changed forever.

A random gunman entered a Long Island Railroad train delivering Manhattan commuters to their homes. The gunman killed Dennis

McCarthy, Carolyn's husband, and critically injured her 26-year-old son, Kevin.

Ms. McCarthy started campaigning against guns. She carried her campaign all the way to being elected to the U.S. Congress. She is now Rep. Carolyn McCarthy from Nassau County, New York, representing more than 700,000 constituents. At age 54, she has been thrust in the national limelight, a TV movie about her is being produced, and she has become one of the most respected politicians in America.

YAFFA ELIACH

Yaffa Eliach collected something far more important to her than money.

Now 60, she was 4 years old in 1941 when almost all of the 3,500 people living in her small Polish town were massacred by Nazis. In one sweeping moment, the village of happy families and laughing children was reduced to a memory. Yaffa was one of the twenty-nine survivors of Ejszyszki.

She and her brother escaped to Palestine. She had hidden in her shoes ten photos of her family.

In 1979, President Carter appointed her to serve on the U.S. Commission on the Holocaust. The gruesome photos she saw of maimed bodies and corpses inspired her to seek a more human presentation of what had happened. She wanted to show the millions of people killed by the Nazis as family members and individuals with dreams.

"After nine days of seeing nothing but death and destruction," she said, "I decided that I wanted to tell the story of my town. What was life like before death? I wanted to show how people looked and lived, but not through the eye of an unfriendly camera — not emaciated and dehumanized, but the way they saw themselves. Everybody told me that finding these old family photos was impossible."

It certainly wasn't easy.

She cashed in her savings and life insurance, hocked everything she owned, borrowed all the money she could, and launched a seventeen-year mission to gather pre-Holocaust photos of her hometown.

She estimates she spent about $600,000 on the project. Not all the photos were easy to get, even once she found them. Once, for instance, a photo of people in the marketplace cost her $4,000, a TV, and a VCR.

The United States Holocaust Memorial Museum's "Tower of Faces"

"People asked me, 'Why this small town? It is some godforsaken shtetl,'" she notes. "And I said, 'This small town will be a memorial to all small towns.'"

Without a place to display her collection of 1,200 photographs, she offered them to the U.S. Holocaust Memorial Museum that was being built in Washington, D.C. The museum gladly accepted.

The photographs make up a permanent display called the "Tower of Faces," which many find to be the museum's most powerful and moving exhibit.

"In this room, you remember that these were real people with families, hopes and futures, not just statistics," says Naomi Paiss, the museum's director of communications.

"I have a great sense of life enjoyment," Ms. Eliach says. "I guess after knowing that you face death, you really accept life as a great gift. We had nothing except dreams. I always say that two words are not in my dictionary: 'tired' and 'no.' "

SUE CHURCH

Sue Church's moment of illumination came when a friend visited her in 1990 and said, "Sue, I think you should go into mission work."

"I told her she was crazy," the 55-year-old mother of two and grand-mother of one says. "There was no way. I had my hands full."

Sue had been inspired early in life to help others. She was a physical therapist, specializing in multihandicapped, mentally retarded patients. "I have a heart for the downtrodden," she says.

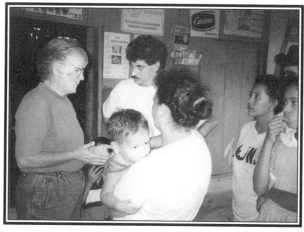

Sue Church of Honduras Outreach

Two weeks after her friend's visit, Sue heard a speech recruiting thirty-five volunteers to work for two weeks in an impoverished rural area of Honduras.

Sue inquired, but the trip overlapped a visit she had planned to make to her freshman daughter at Vanderbilt University. At the last minute, her daughter's schedule shifted, and Sue asked whether there was still room on the trip. She decided to make the trip to Rancho Paraiso her first experience with Honduras Outreach, Inc. Now she is the organization's director of operations.

"After we settled in a few days, we ventured out to the villages in the area," she remembers. "We dropped by the nearest medical clinic to see what it looked like and we ended up staying for hours. It was horrible; the conditions couldn't have been worse. The needles used for shots were so hard that we couldn't even push them through skin."

That inspired an idea. Sue and Fran, a nurse also on the trip, set to work to get funding for a new medical clinic.

To reach Rancho Paraiso, 520 American volunteers a year must fly into Tegucigalpa, travel three and a half hours on a paved road to the city of Juticalpa in Olancho, and then travel three and a half more hours over dirt roads.

Volunteers now find a 1,600-acre ranch with a central building, clinic, dormitories, two barns, a chicken house, and a 28-foot cross that faces the beautiful mountains in the distance. The ranch recently received electrical power and running water. A staff of thirty-five Hondurans works full-time with the volunteers to help the 120 villages and 22,000 people in the valley. Sue and another employee are in charge of the overall operation, based in Atlanta, Georgia.

"The staff calls it the 'ranch,'" she says, "but the people in the valley call it 'paraiso,' which means 'paradise.' That says a lot."

"We don't just give anything to the people," she says. "We work with them to do things for themselves. We work with them on health issues, build pride in who they are and assist them with a realization that they can work together and be independent at the same time. We also let them know that people care about them."

Villagers walk as far as fifty miles to get medical and dental care at the clinic. Groups of doctors and nurses also travel daily to the villages to treat the Hondurans and their livestock.

Under the Honduras Outreach model village program, each of the villages is evaluated on such matters as health, education, agriculture, and economics. A group of volunteers then works with the villagers on a program to improve conditions.

"We work with the villagers and help them get organized," Sue says. "We find out what they feel they need and then we help them get the job done. If they need latrines, they help us build the latrines. If they need a water system, we work together to build one."

"I've been able to learn much about myself in this whole process," Sue concludes.

"I've learned to drive a back hoe, inoculate cows, and do other things to animals that I don't even want to tell you about. I've poured cement and run a cement mixer. I've even learned to speak Spanish. I didn't know how to speak a foreign language when I started."

At 55, Sue has found age not a barrier, but an inspiration.

ERIC SCHONBLOM

Many college professors spend summers working as corporate consultants. When 61-year-old Eric Schonblom was 50 and teaching engineering at the University of Tennessee at Chattanooga, he took a different route.

He started a computer summer camp for underprivileged youngsters in the rural hills of southeastern Kentucky.

His goal was simple. He wanted to touch lives and make them better.

He would someday like to see one of his youngsters rise from the poverty of Appalachia and get a college scholarship to Yale or another Ivy League School. He is now sowing those seeds of greatness.

"The parents in the poorest families see the computer as their children's entry into middle-class America," he observes.

To the parents and youngsters, he is known as Eric or "Computer Man." Each summer, 140 grade school youngsters attend one of four two-week sessions of the computer day camp. The youngsters, mostly from poor families, receive a snack and lunch as well as organized recreation, but the day revolves around two hours of learning about the computers that Schonblom has collected.

The tuition is $10 per child with siblings charged $5 each. In truth, few pay anything. Schonblom drives from home to home signing up youngsters, and he puts in several thousand dollars of his own each summer to keep the camp going.

"It's wonderful what Eric's done here," says Fred Wooten, the clerk at A. C. Sparks Kentucky Food Store in nearby Hazard, Kentucky. "He's giving those children good training so they can learn computers. They're a step ahead when they go to school.

"It's really an amazing story," Wooten continues. "Here's somebody who has made a commitment to spend a major part of his life making a difference in the lives of these youngsters. And not just short-term, long-term. He's been very meaningful to this community."

Schonblom donates his time, and five part-time assistants are paid by the Buckhorn Children's Center, a Presbyterian home for troubled children.

Schonblom has no family of his own. "There's no doubt that this is like a surrogate family for me," he notes.

> *"Not until the game is over and all the chips have been counted can you calculate a man's winnings and losses. And not until he stands against the perspective of history can you correctly measure his stature."*
> — Jimmy Hoffa

SOMETIMES IT TAKES A LITTLE LUCK

Some people luck out in the gene pool and grow up looking like Cindy Crawford rather than Phyllis Diller.

Others are born into poverty or royalty. Most of us are some place between the two. The luck of the draw doesn't end at birth. Fate plays a part in every aspect of life.

Bad luck is easier to isolate and define. What if Princess Diana's car had taken another route or been five minutes earlier or later? What if John Kennedy had been sick and not gone to Dallas? What if a child had not stepped in front of a car?

My friend Tom Mosser had it made. He worked in the office across from mine in New York. He was articulate and well liked. One day he stood in his kitchen on a Saturday morning and opened his mail. One of the packages was a bomb sent to him by the infamous "Unabomber" who had simply read his name in a newspaper article. Tom died that morning. We don't hear the good news as often.

Jack Pyms went bust as a Florida real estate developer. He had worked in Miami for forty years and built one of the most successful real estate businesses in the area. In an economic downturn, he lost it all.

"I had serious cash flow problems and filed bankruptcy," he remembers. "I was completely wiped out. I lost everything."

At age 63, it seemed too late to start over. And he had experienced a tragedy. "I lost a son in 1988," he said softly. "He died in an auto accident just before his 29th birthday. That was my low point in life."

Pyms moved to Denver to get away from it all. He lived in a small house his daughter owned.

"I always kept a positive attitude," he says. "Even when I went bankrupt, I felt sure something good would happen. I kept thinking, 'Never give up. Keep on going.'

"Commercial real estate is like gambling. You have to be willing to accept the consequences."

Pyms won $5.8 million in the Colorado lottery. He's now back in Florida and back in the real estate business.

"I'm 71 years old and doing great," he says. "We live in a condo in Palm Beach, and my business is up and going again. I just felt I was going to win at something. I knew things would get better and turn out OK. I never got depressed over what was happening."

You never know when you might hit the jackpot.

A client once told me a story I'll never forget.

His name was Roy Vagelos, and he ran Merck, a very large pharmaceutical company noted for its ability to discover new medicines.

Merck wanted my company to plan a large event for its employees. Mr. Vagelos described in vivid detail how he envisioned the event, but he wanted us to search for greater ideas, with his direction leading the way. Be like the three princes of Serendip, he said.

I had no idea what he was talking about.

"Look up the word 'serendipity' in the dictionary," he continued, "and it will tell you it is derived from a fairy tale of three Persian princes — The Three Princes of Serendip. As young boys, the three princes set their plan to spend their lives in search of a fabled treasure. This great hidden treasure had many clues suggesting where it might be found. They gathered the clues and set out to find it.

"Alas," he concluded, "They never found the treasure, but in the search, they found many treasures of equal or greater value."

He explained how his company operated that way. His scientists always had a plan as to what great cure they were trying to find. However, most of the time they never found it. But, in the process of searching, they uncovered many wonderful new medicines for other diseases.

The journey through life can lead to some wonderful surprises, and the most interesting ones can come late.

JAMES MICHENER

I worked three years for Whittle Communications, based in Knoxville, Tennessee. I went there when the company offered me a job to run its event-marketing division. Whittle was well respected, and the job offered a good way for me to escape from New York and return to the South. I kept a small apartment in Knoxville and commuted back and forth from Atlanta each week by car. The drive took three hours and fifteen minutes, just long enough to listen to a book on tape.

My favorite audiobook was the autobiography of author James Michener, *The World is My Home.*

Michener's thick books take place all over the world, with such titles as *Hawaii, Alaska, Texas, Chesapeake, Centennial, Poland,* and *Mexico.* He wrote more than forty books that have sold more than fifty million copies and been translated into fifty-two different languages.

It all started by mistake, well after the pattern for his life seemed firmly set.

A middle-aged college professor from Doylestown, Pennsylvania, James Michener had $800 to his name and a war in his future. During World War II, he was drafted into the army, and to avoid ground combat, he decided to enter the U. S. Navy instead.

Michener had grown up an orphan in Doylestown raised in poverty by a foster mother, Mabel Michener, who took in laundry to make a living. Always adventuresome, he had hitchhiked through forty-five states by the time he was 19.

A bright student, Michener attended Swarthmore College and attended graduate school at Harvard on scholarship, as well as several other schools that paid his way during the depression. He taught school but with no particular success.

In the navy, Michener was an odd bird — too old to fight and difficult to place in the normal machinery of military action. Since he taught college history, he was put in a unit charged with chronicling military bases during the war.

One of the curiosities of the South Pacific front was the military bases located on remote tropical islands, away from the fighting.

Because he was the oldest, Michener was sent as far away from the fighting as possible, given the job of recording what the war looked like from these island bases.

Michener was assigned to paradise. He went to the island of Espiritu Santo, where news from the war front was slow to arrive, and the troops had little to do other than enjoy life. This peaceful place offered an idyllic lifestyle in a leisurely pace with beautiful young girls.

Michener, the middle-aged navy lieutenant, made the most of the assignment.

He chronicled what he witnessed, though little of it had to do with fighting.

He wrote about the romance between a young Tonganese girl and a marine lieutenant, and about her colorful mother, Bloody Mary, who sold beads and beetle nuts to the sailors.

He told of a nurse who fell in love with a much older French owner of a sugar cane plantation.

He wrote about talent shows put on by the enlisted men and secret trips to enchanted islands at night.

When the war ended, Michener had his report, but no one in the navy wanted it. So, he kept it for himself. He combined his reports into a series of short stories and talked a book company into publishing the *Tales of the South Pacific*.

The book didn't sell well. But he had enjoyed writing during the war, so he penned another book, an autobiography. The publisher didn't like it.

In the meantime, the Broadway director Joshua Logan was working with composers Richard Rodgers and Oscar Hammerstein on a musical about life in the South Pacific during the war. Logan went to the library to research the topic, and while referencing "South Pacific," he found the book written by the unknown writer James Michener.

Logan particularly liked three of Michener's stories, the one about the nurse and the planter, the one about the marine and the native girl, and the one about the small exotic island. He wove them into one Broadway script, which he titled *South Pacific*.

In the hope that it might promote his new play, Logan submitted Michener's book to the Pulitzer Prize committee. Alice Roosevelt Longworth, a friend of Pulitzer Committee Chairman Arthur Krock, was one of the few who had read the book and recommended it to Krock. James Michener won a Pulitzer Prize for a book that few had bought and hardly anyone other than Josh Logan had read.

"Accidentally my book stumbled into the 1947 judging, the only year in which it had a chance of winning," he remembered. "It found that haven by pure luck."

Michener's advice to young struggling writers: "Make sure Rodgers and Hammerstein read your first book."

On the same day Michener received notification of the Pulitzer Prize that he didn't know he was in line for, he got a letter from his agent noting that his latest manuscript was rejected and suggesting he look for another line of work.

Michener kept writing until his death at age 91. He was noted for getting up early and getting to work on his typewriter. He was a disciplined and prolific writer.

The knowledge of Michener's age and energy for writing have kept countless readers thinking that life can be challenging and exciting well into old age.

"I have kept myself alive and vital by looking into new subjects," he once said, adding that mortality had been the driving force in his writing. Without it, he probably wouldn't have put pen to paper.

He survived three plane crashes in the South Pacific during World War II. The turning point of his life was a dangerous landing at sunset in New Caledonia.

"As the stars came out and I could see the low mountains I had escaped, I swore: 'I'm going to live the rest of my life as if I were a great man.'"

In 1980 he underwent a quintuple heart bypass, dental reconstruction and received a new left hip, replacing what he called his "rusty nails." This glimpse of mortality inspired the most active portion of his career. Between his 79th and 83rd birthdays, he wrote ten books.

In 1992, when he was 85, he said, "I write at 85 for the same reasons that impelled me to write at 45. I was born with a passionate desire to communicate, to organize experience, to tell tales that dramatize the adventures which readers might have had."

When asked how many more books he might write, the old storyteller laughed, "It's been a wonderfully exciting life . . . about thirty-eight."

BUSINESS LEADERS WHO ARRIVED ON SCHEDULE

I'm not a regular listener to radio talk show host Rush Limbaugh. A couple of years ago it seemed like he was on every station when I was driving my car. He talked a lot but never seemed to say too much.

However, one thing he said jumped out of the radio and stuck in my mind.

He observed there were two kinds of people — those who choose what they do from a menu and those who look at life like a buffet.

I thought of myself as a buffet person. I've done a lot of things, and when I get too much of something, I tend to jump to something else.

The idea of working for a major league baseball team looked fun to me, so that's what I did. I thrived on the action and did fairly well with Ted Turner, rising quickly to the top and reporting directly to him. I made some noise, even if I did some things that are hard to explain.

In hindsight, it is intriguing to think that I convinced Ted Turner to get on his hands and knees and push a baseball around the bases with his nose. I also cajoled him into racing an ostrich while wearing racing silks with his nickname on the back.

When Coke called, I jumped to work for the company, thinking I would zoom right to the top. But Randy Donaldson, now a vice president of the Coca-Cola Company, told me I would likely be far too risky for Coke. Someone who might hold a wet T-shirt contest or some other bizarre promotion didn't suit their corporate profile, nor did Coke suit mine. When they told me the list of boring jobs I'd have to go through to reach the top, I decided to get out before they put me out.

I went into the public relations business with Cohn & Wolfe in Atlanta. I really enjoyed it, and when the firm was bought by Burson-Marsteller, I jumped at the adventure of going to New York. I did well there and moved to the upper ranks.

Then, when I tired of New York, I jumped back South with Whittle Communications for a deal that proved too good to be true. When the rest of Whittle imploded, Paul Beckham and I bought the division I ran and now we have Hope-Beckham, Inc.

That's the buffet table of my career. When things began growing a little stale in one place, I moved quickly to another.

It's easy to look back and second guess.

At Turner, I was the confidante of someone who is now one of the most famous and wealthy business people in the world. I was a vice president of two sports teams at age 30 and was a national leader in major league baseball. The stock Turner put in my hands would be worth millions if I had held on to it. *That's one big "if."*

Coke told me they were ready to put me on the fast track. I had stock and lots of stock options. Thousands of people falling all over each other to sell soda pop seemed real boring. Coke appeared a company that had been built, with its future in its past. When I was there, the stock hadn't moved a penny in a decade. Since I left, the stock has soared and the company is now the second most valuable in the world. *That's my second big "if."*

I got paid in stock when Burson-Marsteller bought Cohn & Wolfe. I left the stock in place, and after several years, it was worth several hundred thousand dollars. I got projections each year that showed I'd eventually have millions if I just stuck around. I grew tired of New York and decided to move on. Impetuous me. I took my hundreds of thousands and spent it all. *That's my third big "if."*

All of us can look back and see twists our lives could have taken. People who work to build their business careers sometimes stick with the same company, but most often, something happens along the way. They may leave for something more appealing, get pushed out the door in a realignment or because a boss doesn't appreciate them, or just decide to take another direction.

Now, Paul and I are doing fine. I have a chance to write books, which I enjoy, and work in areas that intrigue me for clients I like. Life's pretty good.

Most people's business careers hit their stride at age 50 and take off or start fading. There is little in between.

Dermot McNulty worked with me in New York. I enjoyed Dermot. He was a quiet man with a warm personality. Dermot and I would take off work occasionally to play golf, and we lived close to each other in Westchester County.

At work, Dermot had a hard time finding a fit. He was named the general manager of the New York office of Cohn & Wolfe, but neither company chairman Bob Cohn nor George Rosenberg, the president, particularly liked him. They wanted someone with a tougher personality. Bob, who is one of my best friends, is very friendly but pushes people very hard. George wasn't so friendly and also pushed hard.

Dermot then went to work with a Japanese joint venture we had called Dentsu/Burson-Marsteller. It seemed to be a dead-end street.

One day, Dermot gave us his resignation. He was moving to London to work for Shandwick LTD, the next largest public relations firm in the world and the largest based in Europe. My boss, Jim Dowling, said that Dermot would never cut it at Shandwick, for all the reasons that Bob and George had expressed concern. He was just too nice a guy and too quiet.

But Dermot did great. He is now the chief executive of Shandwick. I sent Bob a Shandwick annual report, showing Dermot had made more than $2 million the previous year. In the right situation, good people can excel. Dermot got his chance and took advantage of it.

Over the years, I've met a lot of lawyers who hated being lawyers, and doctors who hated what they do, too. I've also seen a lot of people who have remained on the corporate track and complained that they couldn't wait until they retired. Their jobs and thus their lives were miserable.

However, some move out of the pack, and about the time they are passing into their 50s, they run the entire show.

Doug Ivester, for instance, joined the Coca-Cola Company the same year I did in 1979. I left after two years, thinking it wasn't my cup of soda. He stayed and is now head of the company. I don't mind being where I am, but I imagine more people are more impressed with his current position.

Living life off the menu is alien to my personality, but it has wonderful rewards. Ivester and those like him work their way through a bureaucracy of thousands of people, and by combining business, political, and leadership skills, they come out on top. It's the hard road, but the rewards are remarkable — prestige, wealth, and an ample dose of success.

Terry McGuirk, once on the fringes of leadership at Turner Broadcasting, played the waiting game from age 21 until he was approaching 50. When the time came, he arrived in the executive suite. He became boss when Turner merged with Time-Warner.

That's the corporate track in a nutshell. Players come and go, but the basics remain the same. Too many people maneuver for one top spot, and one of them finally gets it. It's a rat race with one graying rat as the winner.

Talent is involved. It takes a lot of solid knowledge of the company and business. It also takes a lot of political positioning.

The chance that August Busch III is really the most talented and qualified person to run Anheuser-Busch is fairly remote, or that Pete Coors is the best executive at Coors Brewing Company, or that Henry Ford II was the best available at Ford. With the right combination of talent, luck, drive, and a good mentor, almost anyone can win. With one false move, anyone can lose, too.

The oddities and intrigue make someone like Doug Ivester all the more impressive. As a poor youngster growing up in Gainesville, Georgia, and going on to graduate from the University of Georgia, the odds of becoming chairman of the Coca-Cola Company were stacked against him. He did it. It proves the corporate system can reward hard work and talent.

DR. JOHNNETTA COLE

Johnnetta B. Cole rose through a system and arrived right when she turned 50. She then performed ten years and was ready to move on to other challenges.

After teaching anthropology at a half dozen colleges across America, in 1987 the 50-year-old was named president of Spelman, the traditionally black women's college in Atlanta.

Dr. Johnnetta Cole

Her tenure at Spelman was remarkable. This college professor with a charismatic personality raised $141 million for the school and won the respect of corporations and institutions across America. She now sits on the boards of Home Depot, the Coca-Cola Company, NationsBank South, Merck & Company, the Rockefeller Foundation, the Martin Luther King Center for Nonviolent Change, and Wellesley College.

After a decade of leading the school, she retired at age 60 to teach again, this time at Emory University.

She tells a story about a little girl walking on a beach full of starfish. She is throwing them one at a time back into the sea. A man asks her what she is doing. "They'll die if they're left in the sun," the little girl answers. The man notes there are thousands of starfish on the beach and her time throwing them back into the water won't make much difference. The little girl reaches over, picks up another one, and says, "It makes a difference to this one."

Dr. Cole was known as "Sistah Prez" at Spelman, and her fund-raising efforts attracted contributors such as Bill and Camille Cosby and Oprah Winfrey. She called her fund-raising trips "rattling the tin cup."

She believes in building friendships that cross traditional boundaries of race, gender, age, and religion.

One of her stories is about the small town of Newtown, Pennsylvania, where one of the few Jewish families in the community put a menorah in its front window for Hanukkah. The window was smashed and anti-Semitic symbols painted on the house.

About twenty-five Christian families in the neighborhood purchased menorahs and put them in their windows.

Dr. Cole has been a remarkable leader of women, and at 60, she is preparing for the next chapter in her life.

In the meantime, "I will sleep for eight hours, look forward to putting on a pair of blue jeans, and calling up friends and going to get a pizza or catching a movie."

BERNARD MARCUS

Bernie Marcus started Home Depot in 1978 when he was approaching his 50th birthday. He is chairman of the Atlanta-based company that recently surpassed hometown giant Coca-Cola in annual sales and posted a profit last year of more than $1 billion. Home Depot has been selected as the "Most Respected" retail company in America the past four years by *Fortune* magazine, and its stores throughout the world now sell more than $20 billion in home improvement materials each year. The world's largest do-it-yourself retailer recently opened its 500th store.

The company started from scratch by Marcus and his associate, Arthur Blank, has made millionaires of more than one thousand of its employees.

Marcus and Blank, who was recently named CEO, started Home Depot when they were fired from their jobs at Handy Dan, a West Coast hardware chain. They had little money but a great idea. They wanted to fill a warehouse with building materials for those who liked to fix up their own homes. They would have everything the home do-it-yourself improvement buffs wanted and at a great price.

"We've made fixing your house affordable," Marcus says.

They couldn't afford to pay much to their employees and gave them stock instead. Today, $1,000 invested in 1982 is worth $152,000.

Blank calls Home Depot the men's "legacy." Each man is worth more than a half billion dollars, and they say they intend to leave most of their wealth to charity rather than pass it along to family.

Marcus notes that an inheritance could be "a terrible burden for some." He adds, "If my kids want to be rich, they'll have to work for it." He plans to leave almost all of his $850 million in stock to the Marcus Foundation, which supports education and programs for the handicapped.

Kenneth Langone, 61, another founder of Home Depot, agrees with the philosophy of building your own success. "Someone once said that money is like manure. Put it in a pot, and it stinks. Spread it around, and it grows things."

Each Sunday morning for years, Marcus has gone on closed circuit TV to speak to his store managers. Marcus's comedy routine and the "Breakfast with Bernie and Arthur Show" have been an interactive way to keep in touch with the people who run the stores.

Marcus and Blank were raised in humble surroundings in the New York City area. Marcus grew up in a tenement in Newark, New Jersey, where he lived with his Russian immigrant parents. Blank was raised in a small apartment in the city. They both know what it's like to struggle.

"I was born and raised in the streets of New York, which is a melting pot where there are a lot of disadvantaged folks," Blank, 54, says. "I didn't live in a house until I was 31 years old. My brother and I were raised in a one-bedroom apartment. My mother and father slept on a pullout sofa. We shared a single bathroom. We weren't poor, but we lived in a very modest way. These are things I've never forgotten."

Marcus and Blank built Home Depot with a perfect combination of skills. Marcus was the motivator and Blank handled the details. "He operates best as a loose cannon or maverick," Blank says of Marcus. "He would tell you he likes to go out and stir things up and leave it to me to get it fixed."

When Hurricane Andrew devastated south Florida, Home Depot stepped in to help its customers. The company offered its building materials to storm victims at cost.

"Our attitude was these customers have helped build our business," Blank explained. "We've been in Florida since 1981, and this was not a time to abuse and take advantage of them."

RAY KROC

Each year a former vice president of the Coca-Cola Company addresses the company's sales force for the fountain department. This group sells soft drinks to restaurants and other places that serve drinks in cups and glasses.

When it was his turn to speak, Waddy Pratt told how as a young fountain salesman, he received a call from a 50-year-old man who wanted to have lunch and talk about opening a restaurant. The man had called Pepsi, but the Pepsi salesman failed to show up for their meeting. Pratt did show, and the man was a milkshake-mixer salesman who was planning to buy the rights to copy his best customer, a restaurant run by the McDonald brothers called, simply, McDonald's. Pratt's point rings loud and clear. Don't ever ignore a call, even if it's from someone who sounds like a real long shot.

The man who called Pratt wasn't a good bet to succeed. Ray Kroc was a high school dropout with a career that included stints as a jazz pianist and a paper-cup salesman. There was no reason to believe his prospects might change in his 50s.

McDonald's alone now sells more Coke than most countries in the world.

The story really started long before the 1955 meeting between Pratt and Kroc.

Two New Hampshire brothers, Richard and Maurice "Mac" McDonald, moved to California in the 1920s and started a restaurant in 1940.

Kroc was hired by the brothers in 1954 to sell franchises of McDonald's. Kroc proceeded to set up a franchising company, eventually named McDonald's Corp., to get the job done. Kroc bought out the McDonald brothers in 1961 for $2.7 million and over the next decade expanded to 2,100 stores. By that time, Kroc was 70 years old.

He was a fanatic about cleanliness in the stores, and he demanded that every hamburger be cooked just alike. It had to be .221 inches thick and 3.875 inches wide.

He also refused to hire girls until the federal government made him. He felt they would attract boys who would hang around the restaurants and disturb the other customers.

"McDonald's was pretty corny back then and pretty homemade-ish," Kroc said in a 1972 interview, describing the original stores of the McDonald brothers. "But the potential was there."

When he owned the San Diego Padres, his magic touch never quite worked. "There's a lot more future in hamburgers than in baseball," he said.

Ray Kroc died at 81 in 1984. His widow, Joan, is a noted philanthropist. She donated the anonymous gift of money to the flood victims in North Dakota in the summer of 1997.

Kroc started with McDonald's after 50 and kept chasing hard until he was 80. Fifty is a good age to chase a dream.

NANCY SANDERS PETERSON

Ms. Peterson was a middle-aged housewife when her husband, John, died in 1979 after a five-week bout with cancer.

With no more preparation than having helped her husband with some clerical work, she took over the Peterson Tool Company in Nashville, Tennessee, the business he started in 1958.

"I knew I could do it because he told me I could do it," she says.

With 135 employees, Peterson Tool Company serves more than 1,000 customers, including General Motors, Ford, and John Deere.

"There was no way I could be an inventor and do the work on the machines, but math was one of my best subjects," she continues. "It's who you've got working for you and how you mold them. I did not lose one employee or one customer, and I'm in a male-dominated industry.

"I'm very, very proud of being able to take something [my husband] started. To carry his legacy forward, to leave a legacy for my children . . . I think I'm the luckiest woman in the whole world."

WAYNE HUIZENGA

I have only two friends who are billionaires. One is Ted Turner, and the other is Wayne Huizenga.

Wayne and I met when he was already past 50, and in the eight years since, he has been my best proof that people past 50 don't have to slow down in business and certainly don't have to lose any energy.

Wayne Huizenga

I had no idea who he was when we met. Blockbuster was the local video store, and being its chairman didn't seem like a big deal. The scale of things he talked about made me wonder if he was real. He wanted a major league baseball team for his home area of south Florida. As in the case of Ray Kroc and McDonald's, he really didn't start Blockbuster, but he stepped in and made it grow when the company had only a handful of stores.

I visited him in his offices on Las Olas Boulevard in Fort Lauderdale. The office was in a two-story Spanish building that didn't look like it could be world headquarters of much of anything.

He was a balding man with a ruddy complexion and an exuberant smile. From the press clippings on the wall, it was apparent he was a big deal in his hometown. And it didn't take me long to find out he was a pretty big deal in business in general.

He started a waste disposal business while in college. He bought one truck and picked up garbage for businesses at night. He'd go to class in the morning and sell new accounts in the afternoon. Wayne never finished college. By that time, he had several trucks and was too busy.

He made his first fortune as co-founder of Waste Management Corporation, the largest company of its kind in the world. He soon made his next one when he sold Blockbuster to Viacom for $7.6 billion.

He then took over Republic Corporation and made it the largest car dealer in the world, operating AutoNation stores across the country and buying automobile dealerships daily.

In sports, he not only began the Florida Marlins, which won the 1997 World Series, but he bought the Miami Dolphins of the National Football League, Joe Robbie Stadium, and the Florida Panthers of the National Hockey League.

He bought car rental, insurance, and helicopter companies and has an assortment of other businesses. He obviously thrives on what he does.

Once when the Silver Bullets were in spring training, he called and said he wanted to attend a game. I thought he would drive the two hours from his office in Fort Lauderdale to Fort Myers. He flew his helicopter. He landed in the outfield and gave a nice talk to the team. It was a big deal for the struggling women's team to receive a pep talk from the owner of a big league team. And it was a big deal that Wayne would do it. The story in the next day's paper quoted him saying he was my "pal." I liked that. He was a good pal to have.

Wayne is a high-roller but also a regular guy. He works hard on a lot of fronts and has earned his success.

Like Ted Turner, he is intriguing to listen to because he has an assortment of business philosophies. One day he told me that business is made up of "builders" and "managers," and that the secret was putting the right ones in the right jobs and not getting too many managers to clog up the works.

I enjoyed the people around Wayne, too. My favorite was Harry Huizenga. Harry, Wayne's father, was in his 80s and full of energy and enthusiasm. He attended every meeting we had and would ask as many questions as anyone. When we printed business cards for the yet-to-be-named baseball team, we made a batch for Harry, listing him as "Harry Huizenga, shortstop."

When we traveled to New York for Wayne to make his pitch to the National League to get the Marlins, Harry was in the middle of the action.

Wayne's bravado was impressive, but I particularly admired the way he treated his dad. Nothing got started until Harry showed up, and it was open knowledge that Harry could walk in on any meeting on any subject anytime he wanted to.

I guess Wayne doesn't plan on being put out to pasture when he's in his 80s either.

MOVING FROM SUCCESS TO SIGNIFICANCE

In New York's event sponsorship business, John Barr was discussed in hushed, almost fearful, tones. He was in charge of the Olympics as well as other sponsorships around the globe for Eastman Kodak. A lot of time and effort was spent on purely "kissing up" to him. The world of advertising and public relations was out to win his favor at virtually any cost.

I had heard John Barr's name so many times from people who wanted his business that I had built a mental vision of what he would be like — basically, cocky and arrogant. Too often, people who have responsibility over large budgets at big companies tend to be jerks. They view their power over money as a personal power trip rather than a trusted responsibility.

I had spoken to John a few times on the phone attempting to sell him an assortment of marketing ideas, but I didn't get a chance to meet him until a couple of years ago. I was trying to get Kodak interested in sponsoring our Silver Bullets baseball team for women.

John finally agreed to come to Florida to watch the Silver Bullets play a couple of spring training games.

My expectations were shattered. John was a friendly and charming man. He enjoyed the Silver Bullets, and although he couldn't muster up enough support at his home office to become a sponsor, he was quick to become a fan of the team. He threw out the first ball at a spring training game and came to watch a game in Norfolk, Virginia, when the season started. That visit turned into several times the two of us would find reasons to talk or meet.

John Barr and family

Not long ago, I read in the paper that Eastman Kodak was having a bad year and planned to cut its work force by 7,000 middle and senior managers. I suspected John might be in trouble. He had already been replaced as head of sponsorships a couple of months earlier.

He called to tell me. After twenty-seven and a half years at Eastman Kodak, he was being fired.

John was clearly stunned. He didn't know what he was going to do. He needed to work, but with thousands of Kodak employees losing their jobs and only a couple of other big companies in the small town of Rochester, the chances of finding something seemed slim. On top of that, he had aging parents and three kids to get through college. I listened with concern, but I had no helpful ideas. He was on his own.

Recently, I received a note from John with a family photo and a business card from his new job. I called. He had taken a job as public relations and marketing director of a facility for troubled teens at "about a third of what I was making before."

But he was happy. He said that when he backed out of his driveway each morning to go to Kodak, he would have to turn his entire body to check for oncoming traffic. "I thought I had a bad back and had lost flexibility." Now, he has no problem bending his back or neck. It was just tension.

"I jog every day, and I've lost fifteen pounds," he said. "I feel better, and I'm happier than I've been in years."

He told me he had moved from "success to significance."

John made a speech to a Rochester men's fellowship group soon after he lost his job. Typically, a handful of men showed up for the meetings. The room was packed that night. This, in shortened form, is what he said:

On October 6, I lost my job and my career, after twenty-seven and a half years as a sales and marketing professional at Eastman Kodak Company. It was not a Kodak moment I relished. Frankly, the whole experience has been a bit embarrassing. Some people remaining there undoubtedly hold the perception that I failed, that I must have fallen far short of expectations, that I probably deserved to go.

That aside, I am now faced with a choice — either wallow in self-pity or take personal pride in what I learned during my career, leverage my skills, and move on. Frankly, there is no choice. I will bear some scars, but I have discovered and will continue to discover strengths I never knew I had.

So how has my life changed since October 6?
- *The house is cleaner.*
- *The garage is organized.*
- *I watch a lot of CNN and CNBC and now know who Judge Judy is.*
- *The dog and I have bonded.*
- *My wife, Fran, comes home from her job and asks, "What's for dinner?"*
- *She and I talk more.*
- *I talk to God more.*

- *I am more humble.*
- *And now we have a financial advisor because we need a better plan to get our three kids out of college.*

Yet the key question for me and hopefully for the others in the "Kodak Class of 1997" is, what have I learned so far from this experience?

First of all, after receiving the news of forced retirement, it may be very healthy to take time for yourself — by yourself — to sleep, read, enjoy a hobby, relax, get your head together, and think hard about what you really want next. I went to a small fishing cabin in Canada, but not everyone may be emotionally prepared to be by themselves for a short vacation.

Next, refocus attention. Life will not go on as usual so your commitments must be reordered: I kept regular office hours at an outplacement company, where I wrote letters, sent résumés, called contacts, prepared for interviews, scheduled appointments, paid bills, and even did some light reading.

I've learned to ask for help. My advice to you is to eagerly respond to friends who ask what they can do. Seek out others who have lived this experience and learn from it.

Also, take care of yourself. Exercise, minimize smoking and cocktails, take long walks, and take naps if you don't get enough sleep at night. Read a book, write a letter. Reconnect with old friends with whom you have lost touch.

Appreciate and fully respect what your spouse is going through with you. While my wife has been totally supportive and leading the cheers for my efforts, I know this experience pains her as much as it pains me.

As a result, give more love to those you love — your wife, your siblings, your parents, your friends, and your God.

Also, vow to no longer ignore those who suffer a similar fate. How many times have we looked the other way when people in our offices or our neighborhoods have lost jobs? How many times have we chosen not to call coworkers or friends to express our sympathy, sincere best wishes, or offer to help?

Finally, consider, as author Bob Buford suggests in his excellent book

Halftime, *moving from "success to significance." Yes, I was fired. But I was also blessed because I can now move from my Kodak success to my own ideal of significance. What I have chosen to do is try to bring value to one of the many Rochester-based nonprofit agencies, one that reaches into the community with the sole intent of helping people — especially kids — who have needs far more profound than I could have ever imagined. True, the salary will be considerably less, but the rewards will be much more significant.*

At age 50, John Barr is moving ahead to a better world for himself and making the world better for others.

THERE IS TIME . . . AND THERE WILL NEVER BE MORE

On May 6, 1954, Roger Bannister broke running's "sound barrier" with his four-minute mile. He did what was considered impossible, running at a speed everyone was certain couldn't be reached.

A month later, John Landy of Australia ran the mile in under four minutes. Within the next two years, Bannister's record was broken sixteen times.

It is amazing what people can do when they really believe it can be done.

There is such a thing as mind over matter. As Satchel Paige once said, "If you don't mind, it don't matter."

"I prepared myself mentally in a very careful and concentrated fashion," Bannister wrote in his diary. He struggled to push himself during the race beyond a point he had ever pushed. When he felt his body threatening to slack up, he repeated to himself, "It must be now."

Believing something can be achieved is an amazing hurdle in life's quests.

Minister Renfroe Watson tells a story of a high school game in which his team played poorly and had fallen way behind in the first half. At half-time, the coach gave his pep talk to the team, then asked his beleaguered squad, "How many of you really believe we can come back and win this game?"

About half the players feebly raised their hands. "OK," the coach responded, "the ones who raised your hands will play the second half." Despite fielding a team with some players out of position and some who seldom played, they rallied back to win. The ones who believed achieved.

I can also think back on brief moments that have stuck with me for decades.

In high school, I thought memorizing poetry and reciting it in front of the class was dreadful. Typically, I'd stumble and stagger my way through: "Once upon a midnight dreary as I wander weak and weary . . ." That mangled line from Poe is absolutely all I can remember of the recitations, except for one.

Rudyard Kipling's poem "If"stuck. "If you can keep your head when all about you are losing theirs and blaming it on you; if you can trust yourself when all men doubt you, but make allowance for their doubting too." One line particularly struck me as remarkable: "If you can make one heap of all your winnings and risk it all on one turn of pitch-and-toss, and lose, and start again at your beginnings, and never breathe a word about your loss."

The punch line is that, if you can do all these things, "Then you'll be a Man, my son!"

Looking at a new beginning doesn't mean starting at zero. People build up a remarkable wealth during years of living. When a fire burns all a family's belongings, the news says they lost "everything." However, the close friends and the wisdom they have gained over many years are their treasures and what keeps them moving ahead.

Regardless of how wealthy or successful a person may feel at age 50, that person is facing the fact that time is running out. The decision must be made to slow down, to keep going at the same pace and in the same direction, or to accelerate into something new and exciting, starting a new chapter when many might say it's "too late."

An American turns 50 every seven seconds. Every seven seconds. That's a lot of people. Five hundred every hour and 12,000 every day. We may feel isolated in our thoughts about our lives after 50, but we are not alone.

INFALLIBILITY SYNDROME

Anyone who has achieved a reasonable degree of success is familiar with the "infallibility syndrome." It can overtake common sense. At first, the person plans carefully and thinks things through. All life's moves are carefully calculated. The thoughtful planning results in success. Then, the person grows older and bolder. Logic is replaced by a confidence that things are turning out right not because the right things are being done but because the person is a "winner." Moves become less calculated, the assumption being that everything will work out well because it has always worked out well in the past.

Late in life, people need to beware. They can screw up. It happens.

My friend Greg Murphy found out the hard way. He walked into a snake pit.

At age 47, he had known only success. Growing up the son of a U.S. diplomat, he lived in exotic spots from Libya to Hong Kong. He attended the U.S. Naval Academy and became one of the best lacrosse players in college history.

His star shone bright when he went to work for Pepsi, then he became CEO of the baking division of Kraft General Foods. With all this success behind him, he looked for an enjoyable contribution he could make late in life. When he was offered the challenge of heading Major League Baseball Enterprises, the marketing organization of professional baseball, he took it.

Greg could not have been ready for what he confronted in baseball. The central office had been without a leader for more than two years and had a reputation as a "flock of vultures" ready to destroy anyone who tried to change it. The warring factions of team owners fought virtually every new move he tried to make. He was quickly vilified in a job he thought would be a pleasure.

Greg Murphy

In the movie *City Slickers*, the character Ed is asked to describe the best moment of his life. He tells about the day his mother caught his father cheating. Ed, then 14, confronted his father who then left home forever, leaving the family in peace. Ed was then asked to describe his worst day. His answer: "The same day."

Greg Murphy lost his job in baseball after little more than a year. His opportunity to help a sport he loved collapsed before it really got started.

"I didn't anticipate its inefficiency," he said. "There were multiple constituencies. There are also a lot of people who say they are in the game because they love it, but they are really in it because of their egos. They like to see their names in the paper."

In reflecting on his misadventure into baseball, he said, "I feel just as young now as I ever felt. It's not what I expected, but I liked getting up in the morning and knowing that what I was doing was more important than selling bakery products or some other consumer product that doesn't have a place in society as important to so many as baseball."

He insists what he went through was worth it. "I would do it all over again," Murphy said.

Greg had every reason to believe he was "infallible" and would succeed in baseball just as he had in everything else. His adventure ended in humiliation, but he at least had the chance to experience the adventure. It was likely the worst and the best thing that had ever happened to him in business.

LIVELY MINDED PEOPLE

Prominent anesthesiologist Dr. Carl Hug says there is nothing he hates more than to hear a patient going into surgery tell him "I know I'm going to die." Too often, he says, the prediction comes true. On the other hand, he remembers one overweight and diabetic old woman who told him she was going to do just fine. "Every day is a gift, and I treasure each and every one," she told him. "I can't wait to get this surgery behind me so I can get on with my life." She came through the surgery fine and was out of the hospital in a few days. "Attitude," Dr. Hug says, "is 80 to 90 percent of the battle."

Lively minded people are the ones who make the most of life, and when they grow older, their joy stands out even more. My wife's 101-year-old aunt Rachel Snow was genuinely excited last week when she was selected to compete in her nursing home's Miss Spring Haven contest. The winner would represent the home in a statewide beauty contest. She wore a brand-new red gown in the competition. We were more disappointed than she was when she finished second. Her excitement was in being involved, and it showed in the sparkle in her eyes.

TAZ ANDERSON

At 58 years old, Taz Anderson has a family history of heart disease. His father died of a heart attack in his early 50s. Taz has had open heart surgery, and he visits the Duke University clinic each year to reduce his weight. Through it all, he remains mischievous, contrary, and devilish in the way he charges into new adventures.

Taz's first career was playing professional football as a tight end for the St. Louis Cardinals after having been an All-American at Georgia Tech. His second was real estate broker and developer.

Taz made a fortune in real estate, but you don't get the impression that he enjoyed the business so much. He calls it "peddling dirt." Now, he is four years into a business he thoroughly enjoys. He builds and sells giant outdoor signs. These aren't your typical outdoor advertising signs. They are huge monstrosities that everyone in town knows about.

It started with a giant peach — the symbol of the state of Georgia. He built a huge peach on a downtown Atlanta building and sold the sign attached to it. The peach lights up at night and has become a landmark in the city. Then, he built another peach — one at the south end of town to complement the one to the north. Next, he converted a building overlooking one of the city's busiest freeways into a giant trivision advertising board. Filling the building's entire wall, the three rotating signs are the largest of their kind in the world.

Taz didn't stop there. When the Olympics were coming to Atlanta, he unveiled a tower in the shape of the Olympic torch and flame. The "rebel" tower was not an official structure of the Olympic committee, but it was one of the few emblems that showed everyone the Games were coming to town. The tower now advertises Sprint.

Taz's signs are way too big to meet Atlanta advertising codes, but he has gone to great lengths to get them classified as "branded architecture." In short, Taz loves to make the most of the rules, and in his case, you enjoy his mischief. His lively, adventuresome attitude ignores any barriers that approaching age 60 might seem to present. Taz's heart is in his future.

IRIS ALFORD

Going away to college is frightening and inspiring whether the freshman is 17 or 70.

Iris Alford graduated from a middle Georgia high school in 1944, then moved to Atlanta to go to secretarial school and find a job. A New Yorker studying at Georgia Tech fell in love and took Ms. Alford north, where she married her husband and raised three sons in the town of White Plains, just outside of New York City.

When Ms. Alford moved back to Georgia in 1992 to "retire," her middle son, Craig, called her hand. "You always wanted to go to college," he told her. "Tuition is free for people over 62 in Georgia. I'll buy your books. Now, you have no excuse."

The youngest of six children, Ms. Alford had dreamed of college after high school, but it wasn't an option. "My parents were elderly, and one of my older brothers went into the marines and served in the South Pacific during World War II. He had to send his paycheck back home to support my parents. So, when I graduated from high school, I needed to go to work and support myself."

So, a half-century later, Ms. Alford's son drove his mom to Kennesaw State University to enroll. She started in March 1993, and after four years, she has made no grade lower than an A.

"It's very difficult, but I love it," she says. "The young people are nice to me, and the professors like having students who want to learn. I'm quite unique. Kennesaw State is a commuter school, so the student body is very diverse. I've had students in my classes who are in their 30s and 40s, but no one my age. But when it comes to taking tests and making grades, age is totally irrelevant."

Ms. Alford's adventure into higher education has led to unexpected recognition. She is featured on a PBS television special titled "Ageless Heroes," and she was asked to appear in a Blue Cross/Blue Shield newspaper ad.

"I told the television producer I was afraid of cameras and didn't want to do the show," she said. "Then, he talked me into it by saying the only thing that would convince me. He told me that I might inspire other people my age to go back to college if they saw me on TV. That did it."

BELIEVING IS LIVING

A common thread in older people who remain vibrant and active is a "belief in something." In some cases, it is a confidence that there is life after death. In many cases, it is belief in a God. In all cases, it is a faith that their efforts are contributing to something greater than themselves.

Some people lose their belief during the early years of life. However, some reclaim it, or even find it for the first time, in dramatic ways.

A 50ish San Francisco businesswoman, Norma Hotaling is the embodiment of the female executive. She dresses conservatively and has a matronly dignity.

She runs a program called Standing Against Global Exploitation, building support for her cause by speaking on exploitation, particularly exploitation of women, to business and civic groups.

She starts her speeches with a remarkable statement.

"Eight years ago, I was homeless and walking the streets of San Francisco as a prostitute," she says. "All along, I had been shooting the biggest painkiller in the world into my veins."

A heroine addict for twenty-five years, she has a metal plate in her head from multiple beatings she's taken on the street.

In her 40s, her life changed. Bloodied and beaten, she had been left for dead in a cemetery. At the local police station, she begged to be put in jail where she would have a place to stay and be kept away from drugs.

A female officer offered the option of a work program on the streets.

"I told her to please keep me in custody," Hotaling said. "I told her I wanted to detox and didn't want to go back on the streets."

She worked a year at the National Institute for Drug Abuse and then entered the San Francisco State University's program for former drug offenders, graduating magna cum laude with a degree in health education in 1992.

In 1995, Hotaling founded SAGE with a small stipend from the San Francisco District Attorney's office. She started weekly support groups for girls and women who had drifted to prostitution and drugs. She currently counsels about 150 women.

Your cause doesn't have to be so large. Benjamin Roll believed in his son, Thomas. Twenty years ago he urged Thomas, then 23, to leave the family real estate business and and earn a law degree. Thomas turned the tables on his dad. He said he would go to law school if his dad went, too.

Last May, at age 74, Benjamin Roll took the California bar exam for the 14th time, and he finally passed — becoming the oldest new counselor of law in California history. Although Benjamin has no plans to go into full-time law practice, he works as an attorney part-time and occasionally calls Thomas when he needs help.

"I say, 'Tom, you got me into this mess. I need your help.'"

Benjamin Roll was featured in *People* magazine. In the same issue, 67-year-old actor Robert Duvall discussed his nomination for an Academy Award for his performance in a movie he wrote and funded, *The Apostle*. He explained how he had written the script twelve years earlier and really wanted to perform the main role of Apostle E. F., a small-town Texas evangelist. He asked his accountant whether he could afford to do the movie and was told "it won't bankrupt you." He did it "now" while he knew he still could.

That issue of *People* also carried a brief mention of Jane Fonda turning 60, noting that being over 50 wasn't what it used to be. Aunt Bee in "The Andy Griffith Show" was 52 when she played the role. And Granny on the "Beverly Hillbillies" was 56.

When is old really old?

I keep going back to Satchel Paige's question. "How old would you be if you didn't know how old you was?" That seems to hold the answer.

IT'S THE BOTTOM OF THE NINTH AND THE BASES ARE LOADED

An Atlanta business leader named Dave Center gave me some remarkable advice. He was well known and respected in the business community. His chemical company was one of the largest businesses in the city, and his kindness and wisdom won him many friends.

A brash, young entrepreneur had just bought the Atlanta Braves. Hardly anyone in Atlanta knew Ted Turner. What they did know scared them. He was known as a wild man. By that time, I was the team's director of public relations and promotions. The wild man was my new boss.

Before each season, the Braves 400 Club, the booster club, has a banquet at a downtown hotel. Dave was there that year, and he heard a group of Braves employees talking with fear about their new leader.

Dave pulled me aside.

"Bob, you're not going to have a lot of control over what's going to happen the next few months," he told me. "Ted Turner could be a complete nut, and you might get fired. However, there is one thing I want you to do. If you strike out, strike out swinging. Give it everything you've got."

Ted Turner wasn't nearly so bad, and the next few years were some of the most exciting and interesting of my life. With Ted, swinging hard was the only way to go.

That is probably the best way to go regardless of the situation. We all have only so much time allotted to us. Making the most of it is sound logic.

Our game situation is different now. It's getting late, and, regardless of how much we've achieved, most of us haven't done all we wanted.

Let's assume we have heard our two-minute warning. It is now or never for us to score.

We need to make every play count.

We have the wisdom and experience to enjoy the game. We also know that even in the most difficult circumstance a "Hail Mary" play works far more often than it is given credit.

As we move to the finish line, let's pull together the thoughts of the people important to this book.

1. Remember James Michener's philosophy of living life as if you were a great person. If we want to be great, it is up to us to start acting that way.

2. As Phil Niekro believes, doing what is right regardless of what others may say makes for a great feeling of satisfaction.

3. Muhammad Ali's desire to treat everyone with respect and spend time with children is right on.

4. Like Ed Barreto, seek new challenges.

5. John Newton's desire to find amazing grace and make a difference is important.

6. Senior golf champ Tom Wargo's willingness to take the next step says that it might never be too late for our dreams.

7. Happily married Bill Noonan let us know that perception is not necessarily reality.

8. Mississippi benefactor Oseola McCarty let us know there is a place in glory for us all, if we are willing to reach for it.

9. Spelman President Emerita Dr. Johnnetta Cole's notion that every starfish counts gives us the motivation to do our part.

10. Finally, there's you. You want to do something special, too. That gives me hope.

My parting shot is simple. It's my "Hail Mary!"

An actuary for an insurance company would say I have twenty or so years left. My time could be cut short, or if I'm careful and lucky, it might be considerably more.

When I was in high school, our quarterback wrote the plays he intended to use on his forearm (sweat would wash them off eventually). I offer you the following more permanent "sleeve." Take a few minutes and write down your plays — the things you want to get done with the time you have left. Then, place the book on your bookshelf. In some future time, someone will open the book and know how we did in our remaining years.

FIRST PLAY: _____

_____

_____

_____

_____

SECOND PLAY: _____

_____

_____

_____

_____

THIRD PLAY: _____

_____

_____

_____

_____

FOURTH PLAY: _____

_____

_____

_____

FIFTH PLAY:

_____

_____

_____

_____

SIXTH PLAY:

_____

_____

_____

TOUCHDOWN (OUR MAJOR ACCOMPLISHMENT):

_____

_____

_____

_____

_____

_____

_____

INDEX